Schnoodles

The Owners Guide from Puppy to Old
Age

Buying, Caring for, Grooming, Health,
Training and Understanding Your
Schnoodle Dog

By Alan Kenworthy

Copyright and Trademarks

Disclaimer and Legal Notice

Foreword

If you have never seen a Schnoodle dog for yourself, you are missing out on one of the most adorable and friendly dog breeds.

A hybrid of the Poodle and Schnauzer, the Schnoodle has all of the best features of both breeds.

As an expert trainer and professional dog whisperer, I would like to teach you the human side of the equation, so you can learn how to think more like your dog and eliminate behavioral problems with your pet.

If you are thinking about buying one of these dogs, this book is the perfect place to start.

Within the pages of this book, you will find answers to all of your questions about Schnoodles, including those you never thought to ask!

Here you will learn the basics about the breed, its history, temperament, appearance and more, including tips for housing, training, feeding and breeding.

This book is the ultimate guide for anyone who wants to own a Schnoodle.

Alan Kenworthy

Acknowledgments

In writing this book, I also sought tips, advice, photos and opinions from many experts of the Schnoodle breed. Thank you to the following wonderful experts and owners for helping:

Catherine Wilson of BHG Farms
http://oodlesofschnoodles.weebly.com/

Mary-Lyn Gray of Kawartha Country Kennel
http://www.kawarthacountrykennel.com

Amy Dillabough of A & R Country Kennel
http://www.arcountrykennel.com

Beth and Eric Krueger of California Schnoodles
http://www.californiaschnoodles.com

Renee Sweeley of Pierce Schnoodles
http://pierceschnoodles.com/

Amie Thorgerson of Simply Schnoodles
http://simplyschnoodle.wordpress.com/

Sabrina Alstat of Sabrinas Labradoodles
http://sabrinaslabradoodles.com

Deb Ring of Wild Rose Farm
http://www.debsdoodles.com

Linda Arns of Pampered Pets Galore
http://www.pamperedpetsgalore.com

Ryan Hodges (Lillie)
Helaine Kozak (Rudy)

Louise Dohm (Dizzy)
Kim Cochrane (Dylan)
Nancy Simmons (Toby)
Jennifer Sturgeon (Stuart)
Peggy Schatzberg (Tiffany)
Dena Holmes (Midge)
Kevin & Juli-Ann Hills (Molly)
Dale Saunders-Winterton (Snowy)
Melinda Pierce (Staley)
Mindi Reinbolt (Bailey)
Gloria Coady (Taelyn)
Sandy Ross (Tess & Cooper)
Barbara Raymond (Banner Boy)
Dan Follis (Boone)
Deborah Downey (Bo)
Kandenne Galbraith (Salena)
Gene McDaniel (Cherry)

Photo Credit: Banner Boy from Barbara Raymond

Table of Contents

Table of Contents

Table of Contents

Table of Contents

Chapter 1 - History and Origins of the Breed

Introduction

Congratulations! If you're thinking about adding a Schnoodle to your home, you're soon going to be a member of a most popular group.

Although not recognized by the American Kennel Club (AKC), breeders have been carefully selecting dogs from different pedigrees and breeding them together. This has been done with much research and care.

Photo Credit: Amie Thorgerson of Simply Schnoodles

Today, the Schnoodle is a popular breed in the United States and in Europe. Schnoodles are energetic, and they are also eager to please, making them easy to train, even for the most inexperienced pet parent. Older Schnoodles fit in well with most working people's schedules, yet they still need be walked a few times a day.

All About Your Schnoodle

The Schnoodle is a handsome hybrid breed that carries both Poodle and Schnauzer characteristics.

All Schnoodles have a wavy coat that may vary in texture from wiry to soft. With long feathered ears, rugged features and an easygoing temperament, this handsome breed loves being around other pets, children and people, making him the perfect candidate for a family dog.

It is believed that the earliest occurrence of a breed that was similar to today's Schnoodle was most probably a breed developed in England known as the Truffle Dog. It is thought that white Toy Poodles (which were developed by breeding the larger German or French white corded Poodles with the Maltese) were crossed with a small terrier type of dog to create the Truffle Dog.

The combination of intellect and keen sense of smell, both of which are common to both the Poodle and the terrier breeds, as well as their digging skills, created a breed that was perfect to sniff out truffles.

This breed originated in the 1980s in the United States (probably Minnesota) when one professional breeder started crossing purebred Miniature Schnauzers with purebred Toy or Miniature Poodles. These produced first-generation dogs, which were later bred to unrelated pairs of hybrids to produce breed lines from many different pairs of Schnoodles.

The main goal of Schnoodle breeders seems to have been to create an allergy-free, sociable, mid-sized, intelligent and long-lived dog that would not be prone to the numerous health disorders commonly found in the pure-bred Schnauzer and

Poodle lines. While writing this book, I came across many owners who are actually very allergic to dogs, and the only reason they have any dog at all is because of how wonderfully hypoallergenic the breed is.

In the late 1990s, the Schnoodle had become one of the most popular "designer" Poodle-mix breeds. By breeding two outstanding breeds, the handsome and sociable Schnoodle hybrid became the perfect family pet.

The Standard Schnauzer

With three distinctively different types of Schnauzer – Miniature, Standard and Giant – that were carefully bred from multi-generational lines in Wurttemberg and Bavaria, Germany, the Schnauzer had a wonderful physical conformation that was kept throughout the entire Schnauzer breed evolution.

This is a medium-sized breed and dates back to the 15th century. The Standard Schnauzer is the oldest and the prototype of all three breeds. The Standard Schnauzer was the result of crossing the German Pudel, the German Wolfspitz and the old Wirehaired German Wolfspitz.

Standard Schnauzers were classified as a terrier breed in United States dog shows as far back as 1899 to 1945. They had terrific coats and stance, and it was because of this that they were later transferred to the Working Group.

Standard Schnauzers vary in height from 18 to 20 inches at the withers in males, and for females 17 to 19 inches. They have a double coat, which is coarse; their outer coat being wiry; and their inner coat being soft. Coat colors consist of salt-and-pepper, or black. The Standard Schnauzer is handsome with a rugged build, and is intelligent, high-spirited and sociable.

The Miniature Schnauzer

The Miniature Schnauzer, or "Mini," was the product of breeding both the Affenpinschers with small-sized Standard Schnauzers. This occurred during the middle to end of the 19th century. This breed was recognized as a totally individual breed in 1899 when the "Mini" started showing in Germany. They arrived in the United States in 1925 and have since been extremely popular.

The American Kennel Club (AKC) classified these Mini Schnauzers as terriers. This differed from their ancestor breed, the Standard Schnauzer. Today, the Miniature Schnauzer makes for a wonderful family companion. He is protective, loyal and intelligent. The Mini ranges from 12 to 14 inches in height at the withers. Their ideal height is 13.5 inches.

The Miniature Schnauzer looks like his cousin, the Standard Schnauzer. Similar to the Standard Schnauzer, the Mini is big-boned and ruggedly built with handsome features. They too have a double coat with a wiry outer coat and a soft inner coat, which consists of salt-and-pepper coloring, black-and-silver tones or solid black.

The Giant Schnauzer

Also known as the Reisenschnauzeer, this is the largest and the newest of the three breeds of Schnauzer.

Experts note that all three breeds of the Schnauzer were bred over time in close relation to what work the owners were doing. All were bred for one specific purpose – to assist their pet parents in their day-to-day lives. These dogs were also bred with climate, living environment and their geographic location in mind.

Schnauzers were thought to have been brought back to Bavaria by Bavarian cattlemen to help with sheep farming and driving other livestock.

The Giant Schnauzer is double-coated, with a wiry outer coat and soft inner coat. The males stand at 25.5 to 27.5 inches at the withers, and the females range from 23.5 to 25.5 inches. There tends to be a preference for mid-range heights.

Coat colors are either solid black or salt-and–pepper. The Giant Schnauzer is an energetic breed that is alert and intelligent.

Photo Credit: Salena from Kandenne Galbraith

Poodles

Today, the Poodle is classified in the AKC's Non-Sporting and Toy Groups. Nonetheless, the Poodle has a history of retrieving fallen game from water.

The very first Poodle is thought to have been crossed from the white Maltese and the Spaniel from Spain. The Poodle's friendly temperament contributed for this breed's rising popularity throughout Europe, most especially in England.

There are also three sizes of Poodles, similar to those of the Schnauzer. Yet, with the Poodle the three different sizes are all for one dog breed, with the prototype being the Standard Poodle.

Poodles that are over 15 inches at the withers are considered to be Standard Poodles. Those that are smaller, yet stand taller than 10 inches are known as the Miniature Poodle. Toy Poodles are smaller than 10 inches at the withers.

Poodle coat types range considerably from long and curly cords to those that are thicker and denser. Today, these are the most popular coats and are clipped into highly sculpted creations or a sporting clip.

Coat colors that are accepted by the AKC for showing Poodles can include blue, black, silver, brown, café-au-lait, cream and apricot. AKC standards deem it necessary that all these colors must be even and solid throughout the coat.

All of the Poodle's ancestors were great swimmers. The Toy Poodle did well with truffle hunting, and eventually breeders crossed the Schnauzer with the Toy Poodle. This resulted in the first Schnoodle dog breed.

The Schnoodle was bred as an allergy-friendly breed. Today, there's a lot of variability in the Schnoodle as a breed, nonetheless this breed remains popular due to their intelligence and cuteness.

What are First-Generation Schnoodles?

First-generation Schnoodles are known as F1 Schnoodles and are the direct offspring of a Poodle and Schnauzer. Either the Schnauzer or the Poodle can be the sire or dam of the puppies, depending on the relative size of both parents.

As a rule, first and second generations don't shed. If you are breeding a non-shedding dog and a dog that sheds, like Goldendoodles or Labradoodles, you can have a problem with F1 or F2 shedding, but you do not find this in Schnoodles.

Although not typical, there are some circumstances under which Schnoodles can shed, depending on the coats of the parent dogs. If you are using a harsh-coated Giant Schnauzer, you run a higher chance of having a shedding animal. If you have a Giant that has the American coat, the Schnoodle should not shed. The non-shedding Schnoodle will lose hair, just as we do on a daily basis. This is part of the reason grooming and brushing is so important.

Temperament

With the Schnoodle being such a loyal and devoted family dog, it's hard not to be passionate about this breed. They're sociable with all family members and friends, are easy to train and are always ready to join in family activities. Most Schnoodles enjoy going for car rides or traveling by car to go on outings. They are an easygoing breed that delights in water play, whether at the beach, lake or your home swimming pool.

The Schnoodle's temperament usually reflects the very best of qualities from both the sire and dam – the two parent breeds. They display an almost human-like disposition and need to be mentally stimulated. The Schnoodle is affectionate and enjoys being around children and family. They do need to be kept busy and exercised regularly. As with any breed, frequent exercise, positive training and early socialization all will provide the necessary groundwork for a great family pet.

Larger Schnoodles, which include breeding the Giant Schnauzer with the Standard Poodle, are known to have the best temperament. Note that the larger Schnoodle may sometimes be difficult to handle, depending on the Giant Schnauzer temperament in his bloodline. As with all dog breeds, the temperament or personality of a dog is always directly related to parentage, so you can have differences with any crossbred dog.

Size

The Schnoodle can grow up to be many different sizes. This applies to all puppies from the same litter. This is the result of the Poodle size variability along the Poodle lines. Size classification is based on measurements for body height at the withers and not on weight, because of the variations. There are five different Schnoodle sizes:

Toy Schnoodle: Height at the shoulder: 20-30 cm (8-12 in), Weight: 3-6 kg (6-13 lb).

Miniature Schnoodle: Height at the shoulder: 30-40 cm (12-16 in), Weight: 6-10 kg (13-26 lb).

Medium Schnoodle: Height at the shoulder: 40-51 cm (16-20 in), Weight: 10-20 kg (26-44 lb).

Standard Schnoodle: Height at the shoulder: 51-66 cm (20-26 in), Weight: 20-30 kg (44-66 lb).

Giant Schnoodle: Height at the shoulder: 66-71 cm (26-28 in), Weight: 30-40 kg (66-90 lb).

Coat Type and Colors

The Schnoodle coat does not usually shed, and hardly any hair is lost on a daily basis. This is great for all allergy-prone pet parents who want to have a dog. Today's Schnoodle coat will vary from coarse, like the Schnauzer's, to soft and silky, like the Poodle's. Many Schnoodles will have an in-between texture of the two.

Coat colors vary from solid colors, such as black or silver, to those of familiar combinations, such as the black and tan version or blends of their parent colors. These could be faded apricot, cream and white, or faded sable with black tips. Schnoodles can also have a white harlequin mask. Sometimes the Schnoodle will develop a silvery color as he matures.

Similar to their parent breeds, coat colors will change as the pups get older, so not even your breeder will know which color or shade your puppy will become when he reaches a year. Rare Schnoodle colors include chocolate, café, red, parti and phantom.

Working Dogs

Schnoodles are great as therapy dogs. They are low shedding and have low-dander coats, which provides an advantage when working with people and being in close contact on a daily basis.

Today, we're still not 100% sure about the working potential of this intelligent breed, but all breeders claim that their Schnoodles are protective of their families and make great hunting dogs.

General Appearance

There is no official breed standard pertaining to the Schnoodle. All the characteristics discussed in this book will typically be noticed in a first generation (F1) Schnoodle. Most Schnoodles will look like the Schnauzer.

Eyes

His eyes are bifocal and tend to be placed closely to one another.

Nose

The Schnoodle's nose has a boxy square look, like a Schnauzer.

Build

The Schnoodle has the finer bones and the build of the Poodle. His legs are also finely built, like the Poodle's.

Mouth

His mouth is similar to the Schnauzer, and he has a square jaw.

Tail

His tail is over-curled and fluffy.

General Health

Your Schnoodle's average lifespan is approximately 10 to 15 years. Nonetheless, his breeding and genetics will all affect his longevity. Health problems in this breed include eye problems, hip dysplasia, patellar luxation-knee problems and Legg-Calve-Perthes disease, which is a genetic hip joint condition.

Many Schnoodles may be susceptible to a few skin conditions like hot spots, skin allergies and other conditions common to the Schnauzer parent breed. These can be easily treated with the help of your veterinarian and a good diet.

As with the Poodle, Schnoodles become more prone to cataracts as they age. They also are affected by heart disease, diabetes, dental disease and other endocrine diseases.

Schnoodle breeders will generally test for potential eye diseases and hip dysplasia, as well as for elbow problems. There are many conditions that can be avoided if the breeder screens all Schnoodle parent dogs for inherited diseases.

Photo Credit: Boone from Dan Follis

First generation (F1) Schnoodles have wavy, soft coats that need daily grooming. Although they have low dander and shed very little hair, weekly bathing is recommended.

Second-generation (F2) Schnoodle coats can be either hard curls like the Poodle's or straight hair like the Schnauzer.

Sometimes coats may be a mixture of both. All Schnoodles that have inherited the Poodle's coat need to be clipped religiously every 6 to 12 weeks.

What Your Schnoodle Really Wants

All dogs have emotions. They feel pain, fear, anger and jealousy and show happiness when they see us. An important role that we play in our dog's life is making sure that we understand our dogs and what it is they really need to be happy. Since we control our Schnoodle's environment, it is critical that we do all we can do enrich and create an environment that is beneficial for the dog's mental growth and stimulation.

Schnoodles also have physical intelligence. They're able to focus on a moving object and follow it. They're able to determine that a particular object they may have moved would result in another object moving, so that they can reach it.

While some breeds may have a reputation for being smarter, all dogs are intelligent and need to be trained, loved, respected, frequently exercised and played with. There is nothing sadder than a dog that's left alone all day by an inattentive pet parent.

The dogs that form the closet bonds with their pet parents are the ones that have been given the time, training, respect and love that all dogs deserve.

All in all, Schnoodles are relatively easy to care for as long as you do your research and know what to expect before you buy.

Chapter 2 - What to Know Before You Buy

Before you decide to go out and buy your new Schnoodle, you would be wise to learn about some of the practical aspects of buying and keeping a Schnoodle.

Photo Credit: Mary-Lyn of Kawartha Country Kennel

Do You Need a License?

Before you bring your Schnoodle home, you need to think about whether there are any licensing restrictions in your area. Some countries have strict licensing requirements for the keeping of particular animals.

Even if you are not legally required to have a license for your Schnoodle, you might still want to consider getting one. Having a license for your dog means that there is an official record of your ownership so, should someone find your dog when he gets lost, that person will be able to find your contact information and reconnect you with him.

There are no federal regulations in the United States regarding the licensing of dogs, but most states do require that dogs be licensed by their owners, otherwise you may be subject to a fine.

Fortunately, dog licenses are inexpensive and fairly easy to obtain – you simply file an application with the state and then renew the license each year. In most cases, licensing a dog costs no more than $25.

How Many Should You Buy?

First, you have to consider whether you have the time and financial resources to care for more than one Schnoodle dog. Do not purchase a second dog just because you think the first one might be lonely – you should only purchase two dogs if you can give both of them the highest level of care possible.

If you do choose to buy more than one Schnoodle dog, it is best to buy both of them at the same time while they are still young. Puppies are very impressionable, and the first few months of their lives are the ideal time to introduce changes and new situations because that is when they are most adaptable.

If you buy both of your Schnoodles at the same time and raise them together, you are unlikely to have trouble with them getting along in the future. Keep in mind, however, that proper training and socialization is necessary to ensure that your Schnoodles get along with other dogs.

Male or Female?

Schnoodle breeders often recommend choosing a male because they're the easiest-going temperament-wise. Male Schnoodle puppies make better pets than female Schnoodles later on in life. This is because males are more fun-loving and have a tendency to bond faster with their pet parents. Males also get along with other pets in the house much more easily than female Schnoodles. If you neuter your male Schnoodle at 4 months of age, they won't mark their territory on your couch or carpets.

A concerned and trustworthy breeder will always inquire about the sexes of the other dogs in your home. By doing this, they will try to prevent you from having two alpha personalities in the home.

Nonetheless, Schnoodle breeders agree that these dogs are fun loving yet dominant, whether male or female, and that the alpha personality will not be demonstrated until a puppy is four months of age. A dominant Schnoodle female should be matched with a home that has no other dogs, or with males.

Puppy or Adult Schnoodle?

Adult dogs are typically adopted through a rescue group. I am a strong advocate for the work these people do, and I believe in rescue adoptions. With some breeds, however, that may only be the best choice for an experienced dog owner, not someone "meeting" the breed for the first time.

Adult dogs typically come with their own "baggage," which won't be a deal breaker for someone who knows and understands dogs. If a Schnoodle has, for instance, not proven to be good with other pets, and you have no other animals, that anti-social streak can be managed.

There are, of course, advantages that go along with adopting an adult dog. You will know the animal's exact size and how well it will fit into your home, and you'll have a good idea of its exercise needs almost immediately. Older dogs also tend to be calmer, and they will already be housebroken.

You do have to be careful with rescue adoptions, however. Try to determine how many homes the Schnoodle has had. If the dog has just been with one other owner, you shouldn't have a problem bonding, but dogs that have been with one family after another will have difficult issues.

It's also possible to get a dog that has been extremely dependent on its former owner and is suffering from severe separation anxiety or, in the case of owner death, genuine grief. Often crate training can alleviate this type of issue by giving the dog a safe "den" when you are away.

Dogs less than two years of age adopted from shelters can have any of these problems, although they do tend to adapt fairly quickly.

Cases of severe separation anxiety that have led to various "bad" behaviors also cause many dogs to be given up. These may include barking, digging, chewing or soiling the house. Crate training is also useful in these instances, but the help of a professional dog trainer may be necessary.

For first-time Schnoodle owners, the best option is, in my opinion, to adopt a puppy from a reputable breeder. You will not only be assured of getting a healthy pet, but you will have an expert to turn to in your first days of "parenthood," when you may well need some advice.

As you will both grow up together, the Schnoodle will learn your habits and routines. You will be faced with the challenges of housebreaking and other necessities of ushering a puppy into adulthood, but the reward will be a dog that knows you and your household intimately.

Photo Credit: Amie Thorgerson of Simply Schnoodles

Ease and Cost of Care

Before you bring your Schnoodle dog home, it is essential that you determine whether you can handle the financial responsibility of keeping a dog. Owning a dog can be expensive.

Purchase Price

If you're considering buying a Schnoodle from a reputable breeder, prices will range from $300 to as much as $2000 (£192-£1278). Make sure that your Schnoodle has a written one-year health guarantee against hereditary and congenital defects. Prices will vary according to whether both parents are well-bred and if they are healthy, friendly and gentle in temperament.

A more reputable and recognized Schnoodle breeder will often have more expensive puppies, especially if they are high quality, and good representatives of the sire and dam breeds being crossed are used. The first generation puppies should be very much alike and all have similar characteristics to their parents. Yet keep in mind that because the Schnoodle is a cross breed of the Poodle, their coat color can change from the time they are small puppies to when they are adult dogs.

As a prospective Schnoodle parent, you will be required to sign a contract stating that you'll have your puppy spayed or neutered by 6 months of age. If you're adopting a Schnoodle, your puppy will most likely already be spayed or neutered, and you'll just have adoption costs to pay. Keep in mind that if you decide to foster a Schnoodle, all your veterinary costs will be covered, as well as most of the dog training fees.

These websites can be good places to begin your search.
Adopt a Pet — http://www.adoptapet.com
Petango — http://www.petango.com
Pet Finder — http://www.petfinder.com

Consider what's important to you when deciding if you're going to buy or adopt a puppy. At shelters you'll definitely save a life and provide a loving, forever home to a dog that may possibly have faced euthanasia. Adopting a rescue Schnoodle will provide space for another incoming dog.

In addition to buying your Schnoodle, you need to purchase a few accessories to prepare your home for your new pet. Included in this list of accessories are food/water dishes, collar and leash, crate or kennel, toys and grooming supplies. You should budget a minimum of $50 (£32.50) and an average of $100 (£65) for these items.

Initial Vaccinations

Depending on what kind of treatment your puppy has before you bring him home, you may need to pay for as many as 3 or 4 vaccinations within the first month. The cost for vaccinations varies, but you should budget for about $40 (£26).

It is a good idea to take him in for a veterinary check-up at least twice per year. During these check-ups, your vet will perform a physical and oral examination of your Schnoodle and provide recommendations for vaccinations and treatments. The average cost of a veterinary check-up is about $35 (£22.75) which, divided by 12 months, averages to around $3 (£1.95) per month.

The cost of vaccinations and medications such as flea/tick preventives and heartworm medications will be about $15 (£9.59) per month extra. The total monthly cost you should set aside for veterinary treatment for your Schnoodle is around $20 (£13).

Spay/Neuter Surgery

Spaying or neutering your Schnoodle puppy is typically a requirement of the adoption agreement. These procedures, however, beyond eliminating unwanted pregnancies, also carry significant health benefits for your pet.

Neutered males face a reduced risk of prostatic disease or perianal tumors. The surgery also reduces many aggressive behaviors and lessens the dog's territorial instinct. He will be less likely to mark territory or to behave inappropriately against the legs of your visitors.

Spayed females no longer face the prospect of uterine or ovarian cancer and have a diminished risk for breast cancer. You will not have to deal with your pet coming into season, nor will she experience hormonally related mood swings.

Neutering and spaying surgeries are typically performed around six months of age. The procedures don't make the dogs any more prone to gain weight.

You can have your veterinarian perform the surgery or, if you want to save some money, you might check out the local shelters in your area that offer low-cost spay and neuter clinics. The cost for spay surgery is generally $300- $600 (£192-£384), with females being more expensive than males.

Microchipping

Even if you have your dog licensed, you should still consider having him microchipped as well. A microchip is a small chip that is inserted under your dog's skin, which carries a tracking number. If your dog ever gets lost, the chip can be scanned and the number used to find your contact information.

The process for implanting a microchip only takes a few minutes and generally costs less than $50 (£32.50), so it is definitely something worth considering.

Food/Treats

You can expect to spend about $25 (£16) on a medium-sized bag of dog food that will last your Schnoodle a month. In addition to the cost of food, you may want to keep some treats on hand for training – these shouldn't cost you more than $10 (£6.50) per month. This makes your total monthly cost for food and treats about $35 (£22.75).

Chapter 3 - Purchasing Your Schnoodle

By now, you should have a pretty good idea what to expect from keeping a Schnoodle as a pet. After familiarizing yourself with some of the pros and cons, you may be ready to actually think about buying your Schnoodle.

Photo Credit: Amie Thorgerson of Simply Schnoodles

What Is the Ideal Age to Bring a Schnoodle Pup Home?

A Schnoodle puppy needs time to learn important life skills from the mother dog, including eating solid food and grooming themselves.

For the first month of a puppy's life, they will be on a mother's milk-only diet. Once the puppy's teeth begin to appear, they will start to be weaned from mother's milk, and by the age of 8 weeks should be completely weaned and eating just puppy food.

Puppies generally leave between 7-9 weeks and are usually weaned before they receive their first vaccines. It is not beneficial for the pup to stay longer, as that can have a negative affect for several reasons. One is that the puppy should not have access to nursing after their first vaccine, otherwise that vaccine is void. Some moms will continue to nurse despite the puppy being on solid food.

In other cases, the mom is too overwhelmed with the size of the pups and the size of the litter and she avoids them. This occurs as early as 6 weeks old and can result in bad behaviors as the puppies interact with each other. Their roughhouse playing becomes more and more imprinted on them, and families could struggle to teach the puppy not to play with children as they do with their litter mates.

Trainers would even highly recommend training and bonding begin with puppies' new families by 8-10 weeks. In addition, pups need to be highly socialized between 8-12 weeks with new people, experiences and places. This time period is very crucial in developing a well-rounded pup.

With vet approval being required in some states, a breeder can place pups a little earlier than 8 weeks if the puppies show signs of being properly weaned and being socially mature enough. Every mommy/litter experience will be a little different. It's up to the breeder to evaluate and determine the best timing for release based primarily on proper weaning and maturity.

How to Select Your Schnoodle

First, you have to take the time to do your research in selecting the right breeder, and then you should spend some time interacting with all of the puppies available to choose the one that is best suited for you and your family.

Choosing a reputable breeder is incredibly important, because you want to be sure that your Schnoodle comes from good quality breeding stock and that the puppies are properly cared for between the time when they are born and when you take your puppy home.

Ethical Schnoodle Breeders:

• Should use high-quality parent breeding lines.
• Should nurture their pups after they're born, preferably in the comfort of their home.
• Never breed for the purpose of profit or to produce as many pups as possible.
• Have a kennel license and be a registered business.
• Handle their pups every day, and start socializing them early.
• Do not sell pups younger than 8 weeks of age.
• Vaccinate and deworm according to schedule.
• Have a veterinarian that you can call who would recommend them as ethical breeders.
• Many ethical breeders will have a two-year health guarantee against congenital or hereditary defects.
• They will also require all of their puppy families to sign a contract stating that they will have the puppy spayed or neutered surgically by 6 months of age.
• Professional breeders understand that you cannot breed any Schnauzer and Poodle together. Only the very best of dog breeds should be used to produce litters. Dogs pass on temperaments, personalities, intelligence, health issues and other traits.

Signs of an Unethical Schnoodle Breeder:

• Dirty living conditions.

- Inferior parent/adult stock.
- Dirty water or food bowls.
- Pups are caged.
- Parents are not available to be seen.
- Poor nutrition, thin pups that have no shine in their coats.
- Do not allow you to see their kennels, or the area where the parent dogs live.
- Parents that are aggressive, fearful or timid.

A well-respected breeder will always give you a list of references. This list should contain the names of people who have bought puppies from that breeder over the past few years. The breeder should also have his veterinarian available to answer any questions you may have about the health history of the puppies and the breeder's adult dogs. If your breeder is reluctant to give you any information related to veterinary care or previous buyers, this should raise a red flag!

Some breeders start the potty training process before you take your pup home. This is an area that is very stressful for a new puppy and owner, and it takes a big load off the owners and decreases the stress in the new home.

Commercial Breeders

Three to four million dogs and cats are euthanized each year in the United States. Millions of pets also die each year from causes related to abuse, abandonment and neglect. We can all help overcome the cruelty of overpopulation by supporting one of the many organizations that promote animal welfare and protection.

Commercial breeders sell puppies for a profit and sometimes do this as a hobby. Hardly any are show dog breeders who will selectively breed once every few years. There are large commercial dog breeding operations that are made up of entire kennels filled with dogs whose only purpose is to breed. Make sure that your Schnoodle is not one of these dogs!

Many of these kennels maintain cruel, unsanitary, unsafe and deeply disturbing environmental conditions. These "kennels" are referred to as puppy mills, where dogs have no chance of play, exercise and sometimes have very little if any veterinary care.

Working hand in hand with these puppy mills are the brokers that facilitate the trading, importing and profit-making from selling these dogs – often online.

Backyard Breeders

Backyard breeders sell purebred and designer puppies. Many of these pups are placed on Craigslist and other websites. These dog breeders often believe that they are doing nothing wrong and continuously breed their dogs without researching the genetic history of the dog or conforming to AKC standards. Most of them do this for money and breed their dogs at home for a profit.

Schnoodle Breeding Standards

Questions you should ask before buying a Schnoodle puppy:

• How long has the breeder bred Schnoodles?
• How does this breeder socialize their pups with other dogs, children, people and normal everyday noises?
• How do they socialize their older dogs?
• What is their exercise routine?
• What are they feeding their puppies, adolescents and grown dogs?
• Who is their veterinarian?
• What is their vaccination and de-worming protocol?

- Who are they affiliated with?
- What state licenses do they have?

Good breeders want to know where their puppies are going and what their lives will be like with their new masters. You should be prepared to answer questions about your home and schedule, your family and any other animals with whom you live.

Don't take this as the breeder being nosy, but rather as an excellent sign of just how much they have invested in the placement of their dogs. If a breeder does NOT ask questions along these lines, be concerned.

After you choose the breeder you want to buy from, your next step is to pick out the Schnoodle puppy you want. Most breeders will allow you to visit the puppies shortly after they are born so you can make the choice yourself.

It is important that you actually go to visit the puppies yourself rather than selecting them by just a picture – you want to get a feel for the puppy's personality so you can choose the one that is best suited to your family.

Some people immediately turn into mush when they come face to face with cute little puppies, and still others become very emotional when choosing a puppy, which can lead to being attracted to those who display extremes in behavior.

Take a deep breath, calm yourself and get back in touch with your common sense. Take the time to choose wisely. People who choose a dog that is not compatible with their energy and lifestyle will inevitably end up with a cascade of troubles, starting with an unhappy dog, which leads to behavioral issues, which will then lead to an unhappy family and an unhappy neighborhood.

Photo Credit: Mary-Lyn Gray of Kawartha Country Kennel

Below you will find a list of steps to follow when you do visit the puppies to make sure you pick out one that is healthy:

• Take a few minutes to watch the litter of puppies from one side of the room – watch how they interact with each other.

• Look for signs of healthy activity – the puppies shouldn't be hiding in one corner of the room or moving sluggishly.

• Puppies who demonstrate good social skills with their litter mates are much more likely to develop into easy-going, happy adult dogs that play well with others.

• Wait to see if the puppies show an interest in you – Schnoodles are naturally curious and friendly with people, so the puppies should make their way toward you to smell you.

• Spend a few minutes interacting with each puppy individually to get a feel for his temperament.

• Give the puppy time to sniff you before you pick him up and gauge his reaction when you do – the puppy should be calm, not frightened of being picked up.

• Check the puppy for obvious signs of illness – discharge from the nose or mouth, cloudy eyes, palpable lumps or bumps.

• Play with the puppies to see how they react to you, and see which one you feel a connection with.

• Always be certain to ask if a Schnoodle puppy you are interested in has displayed any signs of aggression or fear, because if this is happening at such an early age, you may experience behavioral troubles as the puppy becomes older.

Check Puppy's Health

Before making your final pick of the litter, check for general signs of good health, including the following:

• Breathing: will be quiet, without coughing or sneezing, and there will be no crusting or discharge around their nostrils.

• Body: will look round and well-fed, with an obvious layer of fat over their rib cage.

• Coat: will be soft with no dandruff or bald spots.

• Energy: a well-rested puppy should be alert and energetic.

• Hearing: a puppy should react if you clap your hands behind their head.

• Genitals: no discharge visible in or around their genital or anal region.

• Mobility: they will walk and run normally without wobbling, limping or seeming to be stiff or sore.

• Vision: bright, clear eyes with no crust or discharge.

What the Schnoodle Breeder Should Provide to You

In most cases, breeders allow potential owners to come visit the puppies before they are ready to go home.

The standard procedure is to put down a deposit on the puppy to claim it – you will then return for the puppy when he has been weaned and is ready to go home.

The breeder should supply all of the following to you and answer any questions you have about these items:

• You should receive a contract of sale that details the responsibilities of both parties in the adoption of the dog. The document should also explain how the puppy's registration papers will be transferred to you.

• There should be a written packet of information that offers advice on feeding, training and exercise, as well as necessary health procedures like worming and vaccinations.

• Make sure that you receive copies of all health records for the puppy (and parents), in particular what vaccinations the dog has received and the required schedule for booster shots. Good breeders also offer full disclosure of any potential genetic conditions associated with the breed and are willing to discuss any testing that has been done to screen for these issues.

• Puppies should have their first vaccines at 6 weeks and will go to their new homes from 8 weeks onwards. I recommend using a vaccination schedule that is similar to this one: 6 weeks, 9 weeks, 12 weeks, 15 weeks and 18 weeks. Since 99% of all puppies, regardless of breed, are born with parasites (worms), it is recommended that you worm your Schnoodle pups at your veterinarian. Watch out for Coccidia, which is prevalent among puppies and causes a loose stool, dehydration and one very ill Schnoodle puppy. The stresses of a move to a new home may also be problematic for a puppy and contribute to the severity of the illness.

• You should also receive a guarantee of the puppy's health at the time of adoption, which you will likely be asked to confirm, for the safety of both parties, by taking the animal to a vet for evaluation. There should also be a detailed explanation of recompense in the event that a health condition does arise within a set period of time.

Puppy Proof Your Home

Before bringing your Schnoodle puppy home, evaluate every inch of your home and garden for any potential hazards. Ensure your Schnoodle's long-term safety before bringing him home. Be ready to face any additional problems, since Schnoodles love to dig and may attempt digging beneath your garden fencing or wall.

If you have never lived with a puppy, or it has been a long time since you've shared your home with one, you may not realize or remember what a force of nature a growing dog can really be!

Take the attitude that you are bringing home a baby on four legs. Just as you would make sure that all the hazards have been removed from the house for an infant or toddler, do the same for your Schnoodle puppy. I promise, he will explore every nook and cranny, and he'll try to chew on every "discovery" he unearths.

Follow these simple steps to puppy proof your home:

• Keep all loose articles and small objects off the floor – place them on shelves or in cabinets where your puppy can't reach them.

• Secure cabinets and cupboards – especially those that contain toxic materials like cleaning products – so your puppy can't open them.

• Wrap phone wires and electric cords to keep your puppy from chewing on them and hurting himself.

• Consider wrapping your table legs to keep your puppy from chewing them.

• Clean up your yard – put away all tools and toys and make sure there is nothing around that could harm your puppy.

• Block access to dangerous areas inside and outside your home. Make sure your fence locks securely and block off stairs and doorways to rooms you don't want your puppy to access.

Household and Garden Plants

A wide variety of household and garden plants present a toxic risk to dogs. You may have heard about the dangers of apricot and peach pits, but what about spinach and tomato vines? The American Society for the Prevention of Cruelty to Animals has created a large reference list of plants that runs to several pages.

http://www.aspca.org/pet-care/animal-poison-control/toxic-and-non-toxic-plants

I strongly recommend you go through the list and remove any plants from your home that might make your puppy sick.

Photo Credit: Bo from Deborah Downey

Bringing Your Puppy Home

Plan to take a few days off from work when you bring your new Schnoodle puppy home. The next few days will be time consuming and will need direct supervision from you. This will involve using management tools like baby gates, crates and exercise pens. Your main goal here will be to keep your

Schnoodle puppy as safe as possible and to keep an eye on him. This will be a crucial time for potty training and bonding.

Purchase an appropriate travel crate to bring your Schnoodle puppy home. A plastic crate with a fastening wire door and a carry handle is your best option.

Always arrange to pick up your puppy an hour after or before he's eaten. In that way, you'll be sure to avoid motion sickness or a potty mishap in the car.

Put a couple of puppy-safe chew toys and an article of clothing you've worn recently in the crate. This will help the puppy to get to "know" you and will make the crate seem more like a "den" or safe haven. Place the puppy inside the crate and fasten the seatbelt over the crate to keep it secure on the drive home.

The little Schnoodle will whine and cry, especially if the drive is long. If you have to drive a considerable distance, some breeders suggest mildly sedating the puppy. If you are not comfortable with this idea, take someone with you who can sit with the dog and comfort it on the way home.

Don't take more than one other person with you, however, and leave the kids at home. Having too many people in the car for the transition from kennel to new home will stress and confuse the little dog. You want the trip to be calm, quiet and a positive experience for your new Schnoodle.

When you arrive home, let the puppy have a little time outside to relieve itself. Start reinforcing good elimination habits immediately. Praise the puppy when it goes outside. Dogs like to please their owners, so associate going outside with being a "good dog."

Your Schnoodle will naturally be nervous and will miss its familiar surroundings in the beginning. Try to stick to the feeding schedule used at the kennel and use the same kind of food if possible. Put the puppy in its designated area in the house and let it explore, but make sure he isn't isolated and can see you.

Each puppy is different. Some can be outgoing and will easily adapt to being away from their siblings. Others may be withdrawn and shy and have a harder time adapting. From the first minute that you bring home your Schnoodle puppy, every interaction will count.

Don't pick the puppy up every time it cries. You'll be reinforcing that behavior, and the next thing you know, you'll be spending all your time holding the dog. Schnoodles, no matter how young, are not above "working" their humans.

Continue to give the puppy used pieces of clothing with your scent, play a radio softly in the room, and at night, put a well-wrapped, warm hot water bottle in the crate.

Children and Other Pets

Schnoodles do well with other pets, though they're best not left alone with cats or other small animals. They most enjoy being around their human family and being spoiled and fussed over.

If you have children, slowly introduce the puppy to them. This is not for the sake of the kids but for the benefit of the puppy! Explain to your children, especially if they are very young, that the dog is away from its mother and the only home it has known for the first time and is scared.

Be sure that your children know how to safely handle and carry the puppy. Monitor the first few interactions. If your child has never been around a dog and seems slightly afraid, spend time with them and help them to get to know the puppy for the safety and comfort of all concerned.

Never leave your Schnoodle home for hours at a time and expect him to be a happy dog. All dogs need frequent walks a few times a day and at least a few off-leash trips to the dog park.

Photo Credit: Snowy from Dale Saunders-Winterton

Keep other pets away from your puppy for the first few days. Let the puppy smell the other pet's bedding (and vice versa) or allow sniffing under the closed bathroom door – a tried and true method of negotiating such meetings.

Carefully supervise the first face-to-face meeting. Other dogs should be on leashes and cats should be held until they are comfortable with even the sight of the new dog. Gradually extend the period of exposure and calmly separate the animals at the first sign of aggression.

Pets take their emotional cues from us. You must set the tone for first introductions. Remain calm. Don't raise your voice. Praise good behavior. Do nothing to "punish" bad behavior beyond separating the animals. Keep the meetings short and positive, without stress or trauma.

Helping Your Schnoodle Puppy Settle in:

• Plan a routine for when you will walk and feed your puppy – having a set routine will make things easier for you both.

• Set up a special area of the house with your puppy's crate along with his food/water bowl and toys – this area should be in a place that is quiet but easily accessible in case your puppy simply wants to rest.

• When you get your puppy home, let him outside immediately – choose a particular portion of the yard where you want him to do his business and maintain consistency in potty training.

• Engage your new puppy in brief periods of playtime throughout the day for the first few days, but give him plenty of rest – it will take time for him to adjust.

• Block off rooms where you do not want your puppy to go – it is a good idea to limit your puppy's range to only the room you are in until he is potty trained.

• Introduce your puppy to new experiences slowly – do not overwhelm him by inviting all of your friends over to meet him on the first day.

Common Mistakes

Never pick your puppy up if they are showing fear or aggression toward an object, another dog or person, because this will be rewarding them for unbalanced behavior.

If they are doing something you do not want them to continue, your puppy needs to be gently corrected by you with firm and calm energy, so that they learn not to react with fear or aggression.

Don't play the "hand" game, where you slide the puppy across the floor with your hands, because it's amusing for humans to see a little ball of fur scrambling to collect themselves and run back across the floor for another go.

This sort of "game" will teach your Schnoodle to disrespect you as its leader in two different ways — first, because this "game" teaches them that humans are play toys, and secondly, this type of "game" teaches the puppy that humans are a source of excitement.

When your Schnoodle puppy is teething, they will naturally want to chew on everything within reach, and this will include you. As cute as you might think it is when they are young puppies, this is not an acceptable behavior, and you need to gently, but firmly, discourage the habit, just like a mother dog does to her puppies when they need to be weaned.

Don't treat your Schnoodle like a small, furry human. When people try to turn them into small, furry people, this can cause them much stress and confusion that could lead to behavioral problems.

A well-behaved Schnoodle thrives on rules and boundaries, and when they understand that there is no question you are their leader and they are your follower, they will live a contented, happy and stress-free life.

Dogs are a different species with different rules; for example, they do not naturally cuddle, and they need to learn to be stroked and cuddled by humans. Therefore, be careful when approaching a dog for the first time and being overly expressive with your hands. The safest areas to touch are the back and chest — avoid patting on the head and touching the ears.

Many people will assume that a dog that is yawning is tired — this is often a misinterpretation, and instead it is signaling he is uncomfortable and nervous about a situation.

Be careful when staring at dogs, because this is one of the ways in which they threaten each other. This body language can make them feel distinctly uneasy.

Always praise your puppy when they stop inappropriate behavior, as this is the beginning of teaching them to understand rules and boundaries. Often we humans are quick to discipline a puppy or dog for inappropriate behavior, but we forget to praise them for their good behavior.

The Importance of Play and Socialization

Life for all dog breeds can be psychologically difficult because of all the things a dog must learn to live within a human environment. Companion Schnoodles need to live beside us and abide by our rules. These human rules can be challenging for many dogs.

A Schnoodle that is familiar with different surroundings and different animals will become accustomed to our everyday life. He will become used to different environmental stimuli and will have learned how to react and behave appropriately.

Your Schnoodle will need to make other canine friends and participate in many activities so that he'll have fewer behavioral issues. This can be done by taking him to the dog park several times a week, to training sessions where other dogs are present and even to your local Starbucks. Allow for your Schnoodle to have a healthy and active life filled with positive interactions.

Photo Credit: Cherry from Gene McDaniel

Habituation and your Schnoodle

Habituation is when you continuously provide exposure to the same stimuli over a period of time. This will help your Schnoodle to relax in his environment and will teach him how to behave around unfamiliar people, noises, other pets and different surroundings. Expose your Schnoodle puppy continuously to new sounds and new environments.

When you allow for your Schnoodle to face life's positive experiences through socialization and habituation, you're helping your Schnoodle to build a library of valuable information that he can use when he's faced with a difficult situation. If he's had plenty of wonderful and positive early experiences, the more likely he'll be able to bounce back from any surprising or scary experiences.

When your Schnoodle puppy arrives at his new home for the first time, he'll start bonding with his human family immediately. This will be his primary bond. His secondary bond will be with everyone outside your home. A dog should never be secluded inside his home. Be sure to find the right balance where you're not exposing your Schnoodle puppy to too much external stimuli. If he starts becoming fearful, speak to your veterinarian.

The puppyhood journey can be tiresome yet very rewarding. Primary socialization starts between three and five weeks of age where a pup's experiences take place within his litter. This will have a huge impact on all his future emotional behavior.

Socialization from six to twelve weeks allows for puppies to bond with other species outside of their littermates and parents. It's at this particular stage that most pet parents will bring home a puppy and where he'll soon become comfortable with humans, other pets and children.

By the time a puppy is around twelve to fourteen weeks, he becomes more difficult to introduce to new environments and new people and starts showing suspicion and distress.

Nonetheless, if you've recently adopted a Schnoodle puppy or are bringing one home and he's beyond this ideal age, don't neglect to continue the socialization process. Puppies need to be exposed to as many new situations, environments, people and other animals as possible, and it is never too late to start.

During puppyhood, you can easily teach your puppy to politely greet a new person, yet by the time a puppy has reached social maturity, the same puppy, if not properly socialized, may start lunging forward and acting aggressively, with the final outcome of lunging and nipping.

Never accidentally reward your Schnoodle puppy for displaying fear or growling at another dog or animal by picking them up. Picking up a Schnoodle puppy or dog at this time, when they are displaying unbalanced energy, actually turns out to be a reward for them, and you will be teaching them to continue with this type of behavior. As well, picking up a puppy literally places them in a "top dog" position where they are higher and more dominant than the dog or animal they just growled at.

The correct action to take in such a situation is to gently correct your puppy with a firm yet calm energy by distracting them with a "No," so that they learn to let you deal with the situation on their behalf.

If you allow a fearful or nervous puppy to deal with situations that unnerve them all by themselves, they may learn to react with fear or aggression, and you will have created a problem that could escalate into something quite serious as they grow older.

The same is true of situations where a young puppy may feel the need to protect themselves from a bigger or older dog that may come charging in for a sniff. It is the guardian's responsibility to protect the puppy so that they do not think they must react with fear or aggression in order to protect themselves.

Once your Schnoodle puppy has received all their vaccinations, you can take them out to public dog parks and various locations where many dogs are found.

Before allowing them to interact with other dogs or puppies, take them for a disciplined walk on leash so that they will be a little tired and less likely to immediately engage with all other dogs.

Keep your puppy on leash and close beside you, because most puppies are usually a bundle of out-of-control energy, and you need to protect them while teaching them how far they can go before getting themselves into trouble with adult dogs who may not appreciate excited puppy playfulness.

If your puppy shows any signs of aggression or domination toward another dog, you must immediately step in and calmly discipline them.

Take your puppy everywhere with you and introduce them to many different people of all ages, sizes and ethnicities. Most people will come to you and want to interact with your puppy. If they ask if they can hold your puppy, let them, because so long as they are gentle and don't drop the puppy, this is a good way to socialize your Schnoodle and show them that humans are friendly.

As important as socialization is, it is also important that the dog be left alone for short periods when young so that they can cope with some periods of isolation. If an owner goes out and they have never experienced this, they can destroy things or make a mess because of panic. They are thinking they are vulnerable and can be attacked by something or someone coming in to the house.

Dogs that have been socialized are able to easily diffuse a potentially troublesome situation and hence they will rarely get into fights. Dogs that are poorly socialized often misinterpret or do not understand the subtle signals of other dogs, getting into trouble as a result.

Photo Credit: Lillie from Ryan Hodges

What Can I Do to Make My Schnoodle Love Me?

From the moment you bring your Schnoodle dog home, every minute you spend with him is an opportunity to bond. The earlier you start working with your dog, the more quickly that bond will grow and the closer the two of you will become.

While simply spending time with your Schnoodle will encourage the growth of that bond, there are a few things you can do to purposefully build your bond with your dog:

• Take your Schnoodle for daily walks during which you frequently stop to pet and talk to your dog.

• Engage your Schnoodle in games like tug of war, fetch and hide-and-seek to encourage interaction.

• Interact with your dog through daily training sessions – teach your dog to pay attention when you say his name.

• Be calm and consistent when training your dog – always use positive reinforcement rather than punishment.

• Spend as much time with your dog as possible, even if it means simply keeping the dog in the room with you while you cook dinner or pay bills.

Creating a Safe Environment

Never think for a minute that your Schnoodle would not bolt and run away. Even well-adjusted, happy puppies and adult dogs can run away, usually in extreme conditions such as with fireworks, thunder or when scared.

Collar, tag and microchip your new Schnoodle. Microchipping is not enough, since many pet parents tend to presume that dogs without collars are homeless or have been abandoned.

Shy and skittish Schnoodles should have a name tag saying that they're timid so that if found, people don't presume that they've been abused or abandoned.

Recent photos of your Schnoodle with the latest clip need to be placed in your wallet or purse. Schnoodles look different as they mature and before and after a grooming or a clip. Be sure to keep an assortment of photos in a waterproof bag or safe.

Train your Schnoodle – foster and work with a professional, positive trainer to ensure that your Schnoodle does not run out the front door or out the backyard gate. Teach your Schnoodle basic, simple commands such as "come" and "stay."

Create a special, fun digging area just for him, hide his bones and toys and let your Schnoodle know that it's okay to dig in that area. After all, dogs need to play!

Introduce your new, furry companion to all your neighbors so everyone will know that he belongs to you.

Photo Credit: Deb Ring of Wild Rose Farm

Chapter 4 - Caring for Your Schnoodle

In order to provide your Schnoodle with the best care possible, you need to understand his habitat requirements, nutritional needs and grooming requirements. The first thing you'll need is a comfortable dog bed, crate and a safe place where you can pen him up for his rest periods.

Photo Credit: Mary-Lyn Gray of Kawartha Country Kennel

Crate Training Your Schnoodle Pup

Every Schnoodle puppy should have his own crate, right from day one. This will solve all the safety issues of puppyhood, and your Schnoodle puppy will learn to enjoy his crate.

When you want him to run around and explore, his crate door stays open. At other times, you can safely use the latch and know that your Schnoodle puppy is safe from any harm and is comfortable in his crate.

Confining your pup during the day will all depend on what safety measures you've taken throughout your home and garden. All Schnoodle puppies up to 5 months of age should be kept in the kitchen, laundry room or another room close by that has a baby gate for safety measures.

All puppies look for companionship, and because the Schnoodle as a breed thrives on being near their pet parents and other family members, it's best to keep him close by you.

Ideally, your Schnoodle puppy should never be confined for many hours at a time. It's also not a good idea to leave your puppy unsupervised outside for a long period of time either. If you have to leave for a few hours, it's best to have someone come over and check on your puppy and possibly take him outside for a walk and to go potty.

The crate should not be used during mealtimes. It is a place used for sleeping or resting with a bone chew or toy.

Schnoodle puppies enjoy the comfort and security that the crate offers. Crate training puppies stops them from chewing up your furniture, shoes and other favorite household items while in training. This also helps develop a potty training schedule for your Schnoodle puppy. Most puppies will not eliminate inside their crates if they are taken out frequently to go potty.

Don't use potty pads or newspaper anywhere near the bedding area, because it will confuse the puppy. They should only have clean blankets or a bed in their sleeping area. If it gets soiled at all, it needs to be replaced with clean bedding.

If possible, avoid the use of pee pads, as it will make it much harder to train the puppy to go outside. They may run around outside, then come in and pee on the floor. Pee pads cause more problems for the puppy and the new owner. Train your puppy to go outside from the start.

You have two choices in crate styles: plastic portable units like those used to transport your pet to the vet, or a wire crate.

The right sized crate is one that allows for your Schnoodle puppy to stand up comfortably when fully grown and should have enough space so that he can stretch out comfortably when relaxing. Good ventilation is also essential. For this reason, I prefer a wire crate outfitted with comfortable padding.

You can buy an adult-sized crate for a puppy, just make sure you give the little dog a cardboard box tucked away in the back corner so he has a cozy space to snuggle into.

In addition to the crate, which you will use when you are away and at night, you can also have one or more puppy/dog beds in the home for those moments when your little Schnoodle wants a nap. That's one of the funniest things about puppies. They go at full speed until they don't, and then they collapse into an adorable, snoring pile.

Where Should Your Schnoodle Sleep?

Your Schnoodle should always sleep in his crate. Like small children, Schnoodle puppies become tired and cranky very easily. If your puppy is ready for naptime, it's best to regularly enforce this by placing him in his crate and for everyone to leave him alone. When puppies are tired and unable to rest properly, they will become anxious and growly.

• Place your Schnoodle puppy in his crate, and allow him to sleep for as long as he needs to.

• Place the crate somewhere quiet where there will be the fewest interruptions. The kitchen or the family room work well, since your Schnoodle will not be isolated and can still see you.

• Start off by introducing your Schnoodle to the crate for only short periods of time – 10-minute stretches with the crate door open. Leave some treats and new puppy toys inside the crate.

• Slowly increase the amount of time that your Schnoodle spends in his crate. Keep in mind that a puppy should never be kept in his crate for a number of hours.

• Add one or two Kong toys with a blanket. You can always add something belonging to you that carries your scent.

• Adding a frozen Kong toy stuffed with peanut butter keeps puppies mentally stimulated and helps with teething. Never crate your puppy because it's convenient for you.

During the first few weeks, puppies will look for their littermates during the day and evening. Many breeders will recommend that you place familiar bedding from his former home into his new crate, so that he feels reassured that his littermates are close by. The first few nights can be difficult, but after your puppy has become accustomed to his new home, things will settle down.

As wonderful as your home may be, your Schnoodle puppy's move from his place of birth will be a traumatic and sometimes frightening experience for him. There are so many changes involved, and he will miss his mother and all his littermates.

You will need to make this move as easy as possible for him to give him the courage and confidence that he's going to be okay, and to also make him realize that his new home is as safe and comfortable as his old one.

Some breeders suggest using a hot water bottle in his bedding to keep it warm. If you do this, make sure that your puppy does not chew through anything. There are also some breeders that suggest placing a clock nearby. The sound of a ticking clock may be comforting to your puppy.

Photo Credit: Cherry from Gene McDaniel

Try not to bring home a puppy during the holidays when your home is likely to be busy with guests and unusual noises. If your Schnoodle puppy is a birthday gift, arrange for him to come home a few days ahead of time, or even a few days afterwards, so that he's not at home when there's a lot of noise. Your puppy will then have a normal schedule and your undivided attention during a peaceful time in your home. Puppies need plenty of sleep, even after the first seven weeks.

Mornings are always the best time to introduce your puppy to his new home, new crate and other pets and to give him a chance to settle down before any children come home from school.

Allow for your puppy to explore his new surroundings under careful supervision. He will need lots of love, and you'll have to meet his emotional needs during this incredibly wonderful yet exhausting puppyhood stage.

If you already have a few pets in your home, be extra careful. After all, you want all of your pets to get along, so do not create jealousy by fussing over your new Schnoodle puppy and ignoring the others. Share your attention equally between all your pets, so that the relationship starts off well. Much of the future relationship between all your dogs will depend on what happens during the first few days.

With children in the picture, it's important that this new relationship starts off well and gently. If your Schnoodle puppy is your first puppy, it's best to prepare young children with a firm explanation that all puppies need plenty of rest, quiet and gentleness. Prepare them ahead of time by showing them how to touch a small puppy and what tone of voice to use – low and comforting.

Children should never scream or run around a small puppy. They also should not pull his ears, tail or any other part of the puppy.

House Training

If you are buying your Schnoodle as a puppy, the first thing you have to worry about is house training. Many dog owners mistakenly assume that house training is a long and drawn-out process.

If you do it correctly, however, it can actually be very simple, and your puppy could be house trained in as little as 14 days. Follow the steps below to house train your Schnoodle:

1.)   Select a certain portion of the yard where you want your dog to do his business – this will help reduce the amount you have to clean up after your dog and will clarify your expectations when you take your dog out.

2.)   As soon as you bring your puppy home, take him outside to the designated area and give him a chance to do his business.

3.)   When you take your dog outside, you may choose to use a command like "go potty" or "go pee" so your puppy will learn to associate the command with that area of the yard and, subsequently, learn what you want him to do when you say it.

4.)   Limit your puppy's reign in the house to whatever room you are in – this will help to prevent accidents.

5.)   Take your puppy outside once every hour or so and give him a chance to do his business.

6.)   When your puppy does his business in the designated area, praise him excitedly and offer him a treat – if your puppy learns that this behavior pleases you, he will be more apt to repeat it in the future.

7.)   Always take your puppy outside within thirty minutes of a meal and just before bed time – these are the times when your puppy is most likely to need to "go."

8.)   Keep your puppy in the crate overnight and do not leave food or water in the crate – this will only increase the likelihood of an accident.

9.)   Make sure the crate is only large enough for your pu
to stand up, turn around and lie down – dogs have a natural
aversion to soiling their beds, so if there isn't a lot of extra spɛ
in the crate, it will dissuade your puppy from having an
accident.

10.)   Do not leave your puppy in the crate for more than 3 or 4
hours at a time – as your puppy gets older, he will develop the
ability to control his bladder over longer periods of time.

11.)   Take your puppy out of the crate and outside as soon as
you wake up in the morning.

From your puppy's point of view, yelling or screaming when
they make a potty mistake is unstable energy being displayed by
the person who is supposed to be their leader, and this type of
behavior will only teach your puppy to fear and disrespect you.

Your Schnoodle puppy will always need to relieve themselves
first thing in the morning, as soon as they wake up from a nap,
approximately 20 minutes after they finish eating a meal and of
course, before they go to bed at night.

Never punish a dog for having an accident. They cannot relate
the punishment to the incident. If you catch them in the act you
can say "bad dog," but don't go on and on about it. Clean up the
accident using an enzymatic cleaner to eliminate the odor and
return to the dog's normal routine.

Nature's Miracle Stain and Odor Removal are excellent for these
kinds of incidents and are very affordable at $5 / £2.97 per 32
ounce / 0.9 liter bottle.

Go to http://www.removeurineodors.com and order yourself
some "SUN" and/or "Max Enzyme," because these products

contain professional-strength odor neutralizers and urine digesters that bind to and completely absorb and eliminate odors on any type of surface.

Exercise Pen

These are a series of baby gates similar to a children's play pen that are locked together to form a protective barrier for your Schnoodle puppy.

Exercise pens prevent your puppy from getting into places that he shouldn't get into, and they can be used indoors and outdoors. Schnoodles require panels that are at least 36 inches high to prevent them from jumping over.

Always place your Schnoodle's water bowl and a few interactive dog toys inside, as well as a comfortable dog bed or mat for comfort.

Exercising Your Schnoodle

Companion dogs that have been trained to be working companions spend their lives carrying out many complex tasks like detecting scents, hunting, retrieving or herding animals.

Some Schnoodles can be a little bossier like the Schnauzer. These dogs need to have a strong leader in the pack. As we know, dogs need leaders to function properly in their world. So it is very important that you understand how puppies and dogs communicate with us. They need you be a strong leader – if you're not, then you fail your pet. They need firm direction that is secure. Limitations and boundaries are a must at first. Your dog should respect you as his/her leader.

All Schnoodles are thinkers and very intelligent. If your Schnoodle is bred for work, it's best to give him a fun job and to exercise his body every single day.

If you have a fenced yard where your dog can run around, that is great, but it shouldn't be viewed as a substitute for taking your dog on a walk at least once a day.

If you do not take your Schnoodle for walks often enough, he is more likely to develop "small dog syndrome." This is common in small breed dogs – they eventually become very dominant and stubborn and may be less likely to respond to commands. Often people do not give them free time off leash to do this and end up with behavior issues like chewing, digging and barking.

Playtime

Playtime is important, especially for a dog's natural desire to chase. Try channeling this instinct with toys and games. If a dog has no stimulation and has nothing to chase, they can start to chase their own tail, which can lead to problems.

Toys can be used to simulate the dog's natural desire to hunt. For example, when they catch a toy, they will often shake it and bury their teeth into it, simulating the killing of their prey.

Allow your dog to fulfill a natural desire to chew. This comes from historically catching their prey and then chewing the carcass. Providing chews or bones can prevent your dog from destroying your home.

Our sedentary lifestyle is counter to the dog's natural instinct to hunt and be extremely active.

Playing with your dog is not only a great way of getting them to use up their energy, but it is also a great way of bonding with them as they have fun. Dogs love to chase and catch balls, just make sure that the ball is too large to be swallowed.

When picking out toys for your Schnoodle, regardless of his age, don't get anything soft and "shred-able." Schnoodles can be regular engines of destruction!

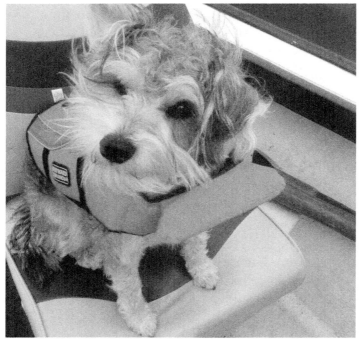

Photo Credit: Taelyn from Gloria Coady

I recommend small chew toys like Nylabones that can withstand the abuse. You can buy items made out of this tough material in the $1 - $5 / £0.59 - £2.97 range.

Deer antlers are wonderful toys for Schnoodles. Most love them. They do not smell, are all-natural and do not stain or splinter.

Avoid soft rubber toys that can be chewed into pieces and swallowed; opt for rope toys instead. Don't buy anything with a squeaker or any other part that presents a choking hazard.

Agility Exercises

Your Schnoodle should enjoy this sport in which both dog and handler are timed as they negotiate a fun obstacle course. Some of these will include ramps, brightly colored tunnels, candy-striped weave poles and jumps. This is a fantastic way to keep your Schnoodle mentally stimulated and physically fit.

Doga

Finding exciting ways of creating fun filled days for your Schnoodle doesn't have to be stressful. Try out a doga class to soothe and relax both you and your Schnoodle.

Doga is great for dogs that have a hard time settling down around other people and pets and that perhaps may be anxious or fearful of new situations.

Veterinarians are also now recommending doga for senior dogs that suffer from stiff joints and muscles. Doga helps by stretching out all tension and tightness in your Schnoodle's body.

Benefits include:

• Helping to resolve canine anxiety and depression
• Socialization with other dogs and people
• Reduces stress
• Lowers blood pressure in your Schnoodle
• Aids digestion
• Same physical benefits for pet parents and dogs alike

Hide-and-Seek

Hide-and-seek allows for your Schnoodle to use his doggie instincts in hunting and exploring. While playing with humans, he'll be hunting for that special toy or treat. This is a wonderful way for him to focus, pay attention to where you are and respond to his name. Children are encouraged to participate in this delightful family game. It's also a great game to do over the holidays, when you can hide your Schnoodle's gifts with your children and then watch as he finds them.

• Have someone hold your Schnoodle and go behind a couch or doorway.
• When your Schnoodle can no longer see you, someone will tell your Schnoodle to find you. He's then released.
• When your Schnoodle becomes good at this game, you can use toys and treats. You can also hide farther away, but don't shut the doors.

Interactive Dog Toys and Intelligence

Have you ever thought about how you could increase your Schnoodle's intelligence? With so many different toy designs on the market, Schnoodle pet parents are able to choose games from easy to more advanced. Once your dog has mastered the necessary skills, he can move on to the next level. These toys are fun for both you and your Schnoodle.

Nina Ottosson has created one of the best dog treat mazes. Here, your Schnoodle has to get to the treats that are inside by making the puzzle wobble, rock and spin. When he does this, the treats travel through the maze and then come out at the top or bottom.

Never use puzzle toys for feeding your Schnoodle, because they have minimal room to store dog food and don't store enough food for a complete meal. Use puzzle toys for treats, especially at the beginning, so that your Schnoodle is encouraged to continue.

Nonetheless, don't choose one that is too difficult or too easy. In these cases, your Schnoodle may sometimes give up because they are frustrated or simply become bored when it's too easy.

The Kong is enjoyed by all dog breeds and can be sealed with an organic salmon broccoli paste and stuffed with organic vegetables and grilled chicken bits.

Aikiou's interactive canine feeders contain over a dozen different compartments. In this case, your furry companion has to use his paws and his sense of smell to find the food that is hidden inside.

Standard Leash or Retractable?

The decision to buy a standard, fixed-length leash or a retractable lead is up to you. Do bear in mind that some facilities like groomers, vet clinics and dog daycares ask that you not bring your animal in on a retractable lead, as the long line represents a trip and fall hazard for other human clients.

Fixed length leashes can cost as little as $5 / £2.97, while retractable leads are typically less than $15 / £8.91.

It won't be long before your Schnoodle associates the lead with positive outings and adventures with you. Don't be surprised if your dog picks the leash up and brings it to you, which is a pretty clear message: "Let's go!"

Some Tips on Walking Your Dog

Because walks and going out are things that dogs enjoy and because your pet will want to please you, you can instill some good behaviors on command around the whole process. Teach your dog the "sit" command by using the word and making a downward pointing motion with your finger or the palm of your hand.

Reward the dog with a treat each time he performs correctly. Then pair the sit command with the pleasure of a walk by refusing to attach the lead to the harness until your pet sits. Make attaching the leash and saying "Okay, let's go!" be the reward.

Any time the dog tries to pull you or jerk at the leash, stop the walk, pick up the dog and start over with the sit command. Praise and reward the dog for walking properly at the end of the lead and for stopping when you stop. The more than you can reinforce the walk as a shared activity, the quieter and more calm your dog will be.

Your dog's main sense is scent, which is why when you take them for a walk they spend a lot of time sniffing everything. They gather an amazing amount of information, such as being able to determine which dogs were recently in the area, their gender, their current health and age. Incredible!

When two dogs meet, they are likely to go up to each other and sniff near each other's jaw and then around the rear-end area.

Have you ever visited a friend and their dog has come up to you and sniffed your groin area? This may have caused some embarrassment, but this is simply a dog's way of learning about you by picking up scents.

Puppy Nutrition

Dogs require a graduated program of nutrition as they age. Puppies of four months or less should receive four small meals a day. From age four to eight months, switch to three meals per day and then twice daily feedings at eight months and older.

Put your puppy's food down for approximately 10-20 minutes and then take it back up again. Do not use the practice of "free feeding," which is leaving dry food out for the dog at all times.

Use only a high-quality, premium, dry puppy food, preferably whatever the dog was used to eating at the kennel. Switching foods can lead to gastrointestinal upset, so try to maintain the dog's existing routine in so much as it is possible to do so.

Always read the label on any food you purchase to ensure that the first items listed are meat, fishmeal or whole grains. You do not want to use a food that contains large amounts of cornmeal or meat by-products. These "filler foods" are low in nutritional value and increase the amount of waste the dog will produce per day, as well as adding to flatulence problems.

Wet foods can cause digestive issues with Schnoodle puppies and may not have the correct nutritional balance for your growing dog. Wet foods are also more difficult to measure.

Portion control is extremely important with this breed. Measure the dry food you offer your dog and use only the recommended portion based on the puppy's weight.

Food and Water Bowls

You'll need to get two medium sized bowls, one for fresh water and one for food. Two sets are always best, so that you can keep a set for outdoors. Make sure that you get sturdy dog bowls that do not tip over when your Schnoodle is eating.

Feeders with stainless steel bowls for both food and water are typically available for less than $25 / £14.87. Stainless steel is best because it is easy to clean and does not harbor bacteria like plastic or ceramic dishes can. Just be aware that some puppies can get scared by seeing their reflection in the dish and will then not want to eat or drink from the dish.

Many Schnoodle owners prefer using elevated bowl stands. This allows for your pooch to be closer to the bowl so that he does not have to lean down when eating. Veterinarians prefer this method since it prevents bloat and aids with your dog's digestion.

Photo Credit: Rudy from Helaine Kozak

Nutritional Needs

Protein, fats, carbohydrates, fiber, vitamins, minerals and fresh water are all part of a healthy and balanced diet for dogs. A well-fed dog needs to eat a wide variety of assorted fresh foods to get a healthy range and balance of vitamins and minerals.

Always try to choose high-quality, easily digestible ingredients that will provide a great starting point for your canine companion to ensure that he reaps adequate nourishment for his brain and body.

Read the labels and understand what's inside your dog food. The Association of American Feed Control (AAFCO) sets the standards for pet food's nutritional and ingredient content.

Dogs, like all animals, require a balanced diet made up of carbohydrates, protein and fat. It is important that you understand, however, that the ideal ratio of these nutrients is different for dogs than it is for other animals like cats, or even humans.

Below you will find a brief explanation of why each of these nutrients is essential for your Schnoodle:

Protein – You have probably heard that proteins are the building blocks of healthy tissues and organs, so you can see why they are such an important part of a Schnoodle's diet.

The best protein sources for your dog include chicken, beef, turkey, lamb, fish and eggs – protein can also be found in certain vegetables and soy, but these are not the best sources of protein for your dog.

Fats – Fats provide your dog with a highly concentrated source of energy – this is especially important for small breed dogs like Schnoodles because they burn energy at a higher rate than large breed dogs.

Fats are also essential because they help your dog's body to absorb fat-soluble vitamins and play a role in insulating his organs. Some of the most important essential fatty acids for dogs include linoleic acid, omega-3 fatty acids and omega-6 fatty acids.

Carbohydrates – These nutrients provide energy for your dog's tissues, and they also provide fiber, which is essential for digestive health.

Some of the best sources of fiber for your dog include beet pulp and rice. It is important to note that while your dog's diet should contain carbohydrates, fats and protein are the most important nutrients.

Water – Another important nutrient your Schnoodle needs is water. You should plan to provide your Schnoodle with unlimited access to fresh water on a daily basis. Have at least one large bowl of fresh water placed somewhere your Schnoodle can easily access it and refill the bowl as needed throughout the day.

Water is also an important element of your dog's food – most commercial dry foods contain as much as 10% water, and wet foods contain more.

Other Nutrients – In addition to these basic nutrients, your dog also requires various vitamins and minerals to remain healthy. Vitamins are the catalysts your dog's body needs for enzyme reactions, and because most vitamins can't be synthesized, your dog needs to get them through his diet.

The same is true for minerals – they cannot be synthesized by the body, but they are essential for maintaining fluid balance and play a role in many essential metabolic reactions in the body.

The BARF Diet

This is available in the refrigerator or freezer section in the pet food area of grocery stores. The BARF diet (Biologically Appropriate Raw Food Diet) was first developed by a veterinarian, Dr. Ian Billinghurst. The BARF diet contains thoroughly ground raw and meaty bones, raw vegetables, raw offal and supplements.

• Many veterinarians have claimed that this diet helps dogs with skin disorders and those who are allergic to grain, preservatives and other added ingredients found in commercial brands.

• There has also been some negative feedback about this diet, such as the threat of Salmonella and E.Coli strains.

• The BARF diet should not be fed to young puppies. As with all nutritional concerns, it's best to contact your veterinarian for advice on a balanced diet for your Schnoodle.

The Dehydrated Diet

Dehydrated dog food comes in both raw and cooked forms, and these foods are usually air-dried to reduce moisture to the level where bacterial growth is inhibited.

The appearance of dehydrated dog food is very similar to dry kibble, and the typical feeding methods include adding warm water before serving, which makes this type of diet both healthy for our dogs and convenient for us to serve.

Dehydrated recipes are made from minimally processed fresh whole foods to create a healthy and nutritionally balanced meal that will meet or exceed the dietary requirements for healthy canines.

Dehydrating removes only the moisture from the fresh ingredients, which usually means that because the food has not already been cooked at a high temperature, more of the overall nutrition is retained.

A dehydrated diet is a convenient way to feed your dog a nutritious diet, because all you have to do is add warm water and wait five minutes while the food re-hydrates so your Schnoodle can enjoy a warm meal.

The Kibble Diet

There is no mistaking that the convenience and relative economy of dry dog food kibble, which had its beginnings in the 1940s, continues to make it the most popular pet food choice for most humans.

While feeding a high-quality, bagged kibble diet that has been flavored to appeal to dogs and supplemented with vegetables and fruits to appeal to humans may keep most every Schnoodle dog companion happy and healthy, you will need to decide whether this is the best diet for them.

Choosing a Dog Food

Opt for organic, well-balanced diets that have been recommended by your veterinarian. What really matters most is that you choose the correct puppy food for your Schnoodle.

There are special puppy foods especially formulated for Toy breeds, large dogs, medium breeds, and giant puppies like the Great Dane. The majority of puppies will grow to their full size within one year. During this stage they will benefit from a balanced diet, so that they can grow into healthy adult Schnoodles.

Next, you will find some tips to help you choose a commercial dog food formula that will provide for your Schnoodle's nutritional and energy needs:

• The first ingredient on the list should be a whole meat source – chicken, not chicken meal (and certainly not some other product like corn or wheat).

• Select a formula that is designed for small breed dogs, because the pieces will be smaller and easier for your Schnoodle to eat.

• Compare the fat content of various formulas – small breeds like Schnoodles require more fat for energy than large breed dogs.

• Look for easily digestible sources of carbohydrate on the ingredients list – things like cooked rice, oats and barley.

• Consider avoiding common allergens in dog foods like wheat and corn.

• Look for an AAFCO statement of nutritional adequacy on the package – this states that the food meets certain nutritional requirements.

• Check to be sure that the food contains at least 18% (dry matter) protein for adult dogs and 22% for puppies and pregnant/lactating females.

• Look for a food that provides at least 5% (dry matter) fat for adult dogs and 8% for puppies and pregnant/lactating females.

Note: Most dog food packages list the amounts of specific nutrients in the Guaranteed Analysis. Unfortunately, most of these list foods expressed in an "as fed" basis, which can be misleading – a more accurate measurement is dry matter.

To find the dry matter content of a food, look at the moisture content of the food and subtract that from 100%. For example, a food that has 10% moisture has 90% dry matter. Then, divide the "as fed" amount of each nutrient by that 90% to find the dry matter content of each nutrient.

What Should I Never Feed My Schnoodle?

There is probably not a dog owner on earth who can say that he never fed his dog scraps from the table or dropped him a "treat" once in a while. It is important to realize, however, that there are some foods that you may not know are harmful for Schnoodles:

Alcohol
Apple seeds
Avocado
Cherry pits
Candy
Chocolate
Coffee
Garlic
Grapes
Gum
Hops
Macadamia nuts
Mushroom
Mustard seeds
Onions
Peach pits
Potato stems
Raisins
Salt
Tea
Tomato leaves
Walnuts

Xylitol
Yeast

If you allow your puppy to chew on a bone, monitor the dog closely. Use only small knuckle or joint bones. Remove the item at the first sign of splintering. Most owners prefer commercial chew toys that are rated "puppy safe."

Photo Credit: Linda Arns of Pampered Pets Galore

Best Seafood for Schnoodles

Seafood is loaded with protein, minerals and enzymes when fresh and also has lots of collagen. Spirulina and chlorella are a more concentrated source of chlorophylls than any other food. Both of these algae help reduce inflammation and are also rich in essential fatty acids.

Organic Salmon Patties With Spinach

1 ¼ pounds organic salmon fillet
2 cups organic whole wheat bread crumbs
1 large organic brown egg
1 bunch organic spinach pureed – trimmed
1 organic celery stalk, cubed without the string
2 tablespoons chopped organic parsley – no stalks
1 tablespoon organic olive oil

• Combine all the ingredients, except for the olive oil, in a bowl. Mix well.
• Cover and refrigerate for up to 3 hours or until the mixture is firm.
• Shape the salmon mixture into medium-sized patties or different fun shapes. You can use a cookie cutter for this. Schnoodles enjoy the different shapes.
• Heat the olive oil over medium heat. Add patties and brown until cooked on both sides. Each side should take 2-3 minutes.
• Remove from skillet and allow to cool.
• Serve. This can be added to brown rice, quinoa or couscous and topped with a dollop of plain yogurt and blueberries.

Vegetable and Fruit Treats

All green organic and natural produce like fresh broccoli, baby carrots, asparagus and celery are appealing to Schnoodles and great to use as treats. These crunchy vegetables are extremely nutritious and low in calories, so dogs can enjoy these to their heart's content.

Baked Organic Kale Frittata Treats

One medium bunch of green organic kale, chopped into small, bite-size pieces

1 tsp. olive oil
Pinch of organic sea salt
6 organic cage-free eggs
½ -cup organic milk
½ -cup organic shredded cheese – mild cheddar

Preheat oven to 400 degrees Fahrenheit. Grease a muffin pan. Chop the organic kale and lightly sauté over medium to low heat. Cook for 3 minutes or until the kale is tender. Set aside until very cooled.

In a medium-sized bowl, whisk the eggs and milk. Stir in the cheese and kale. Transfer into the muffin cups, filling them halfway.

Bake for 15 minutes or until golden brown. Always cool before serving. Enjoy with your Schnoodle!

Organic Diets

For many of us today, feeding our families an organic diet that is wholesome and nutritionally complete has become a priority. Today, many pet parents are doing this for their dogs as well.

By investing just a little time and effort to make organic and natural homemade meals ourselves, our dogs have shinier coats, much more energy, less allergy problems and many other benefits. Schnoodle parents have the convenience of thawing and then serving organic meals and in turn knowing that the diet we're feeding our Schnoodles is complete and balanced, with the right combination of vitamins, minerals and nutrients.

Your Schnoodle will love:

Cooked organic boneless chicken pieces

Organic, homemade cookies
Cheerios
Raw organic carrots
Hard-boiled organic eggs
Organic string cheese or mild cubed cheddar cheese
Sardines – low salt
Organic dog treats (not from China)
Organic popcorn
Organic rice cakes
Organic fish balls
Organic cooked hamburger pieces
Organic turkey hotdogs
Blueberries

Grooming

All dog breeds need daily grooming, veterinary care, daily exercise and plenty of consistent positive training. Schnoodles are no exception. They too need lots of grooming and exercise.

If you keep your Schnoodle's coat very short, it will help you to keep an eye on any skin conditions that your dog may have. A clipped coat will last anywhere from 2-4 months and will keep your Schnoodle comfortable if you live in a humid or hot country.

Your Schnoodle should also be bathed at least once a month with organic dog products. This can be done easily at the groomers or at home in your tub.

Grooming every day will prevent tangles and mats from forming in his coat. Your Schnoodle puppy needs to associate grooming with love, fun and kindness. Any form of grooming has to be done gently.

Do not allow yourself to get caught in the "my Schnoodle doesn't like it" trap, which is an excuse many owners will use to avoid regular grooming sessions. When you allow your dog to dictate whether they will permit a grooming session, you are setting a dangerous precedent.

Once you have bonded with your dog, they love to be tickled, rubbed and scratched in certain favorite places. This is why grooming is a great source of pleasure and a way to bond with your pet.

The Schnoodle breed is very popular today. Everyone wants a "look" that clearly says Schnoodle. Nonetheless, many groomers either do a Poodle or a Schnauzer clip. Schnoodles do best with their own Schnoodle look. Before taking your Schnoodle to the groomers, make sure that he has his own unique "Schnoodle" clip.

Daily grooming is a must with Schnoodles. You'll need to comb your dog's body with a steel dog comb, which can be bought from any pet store or online. The dog comb gets rid of all tangles right down to your Schnoodle's skin. Brushes are wonderful for brushing and fast touch-ups, yet they do not remove the tangles; and if you only brush, you'll end up with tangles and mats that may be impossible to remove.

Necessary Grooming Supplies

• Bristle brush: This is used to take off any excess hair after grooming. Great to use on your Schnoodle's belly and legs.

• Slicker Brush: A slicker brush should be the first tool in your grooming kit. They come in different sizes and shapes. The gentle slicker brush has softer wire bristles and is best on puppies and small breeds.

• Pin Brush: A pin brush works best on breeds with short coats.

• Rubber Curry Comb: The curry comb fits into your palm and contains flexible rubber nibs. It works by loosening your Schnoodle's undercoat and brings all the grime to the surface of your Schnoodle's coat.

• Organic or Natural Shampoo: Schnoodles do best with an organic or natural, chemical-free shampoo. Since they are prone to skin sensitivities, dry skin or flaky skin, it's best not to wash your Schnoodle every week. Take your dog to the veterinarian if he has any unusual lumps or skin irritations.

• Dematter: This breaks up mats and removes knots.

• Toothbrush: Make choosing a doggie toothbrush a priority in your Schnoodle's health care. Fingertip brushes work well for Schnoodle puppies, while the standard canine toothbrush works well for adult dogs.

• Special dog toothpastes like the meat-flavored ones are especially made for dogs. This makes it so much easier for your Schnoodle to tolerate and perhaps enjoy having his teeth brushed. Human toothpaste should never be used on dogs.

• Nail Clippers: These are usually guillotine shaped in style and have a sharp blade that squeezes shut. Alternative name brands include the Dremel or a similar tool that would grind down your dog's nail instead of cutting it.

Tips for Bathing and Rinsing Your Schnoodle

It takes a few minutes of prep time to organize everything you'll need. Before you begin with bathing, gather all your supplies and have them right next to you. Try to always use a natural or organic dog shampoo and conditioner.

Step One

Place the cotton balls for inner ear protection, a washcloth or two, blow dryer and a few soft cotton towels around you. Before starting off, it's necessary to brush out all the excess hair from your Schnoodle's coat.

Your veterinarian will have most likely recommended some eye drops to place in your dog's eyes before bathing. This will protect his eyes from any irritation that is often caused from shampoo. Gently place the eye drops in your dog's eyes. Next, place a cotton ball in each ear, so as to prevent water from entering, and to protect against ear infections.

Photo Credit: Amie Thorgerson of Simply Schnoodles

Step Two

Now, keep your Schnoodle close to you and as comfortable as possible. This is a good time to play some classical music. Dogs are less tolerant of water that is too warm for them, more so than their pet parents, so it's important that your water is lukewarm.

If your Schnoodle starts shivering and seems cold, check your water temperature. Soak him gently with the warm water. Always check the temperature by allowing for the water to run against your wrist first before running the water over your Schnoodle. In this way, you'll avoid any accidents. Then make sure that he's soaked all the way through to his skin.

Step Three

Schnoodles that suffer from hip dysplasia or arthritic problems may have a harder time with bathing. If they have to lie down, be gentle and gently alternate sides by placing them on a few large cotton towels that are easy to move.

Be careful never to submerge his head, ears or even neck area. The water level should be kept low to minimize drowning risk, ear infections and to avoid a simple overflow.

Make this a fun task that is relaxing for both you and your Schnoodle. If this is your puppy's first shampoo, it's important that this be a positive experience for him so that he'll learn to enjoy bathing and grooming at home.

Step Four

Finally, work the organic shampoo into your Schnoodle's coat and gently lather him all over. Swirl the lather against the grain, so as to make his coat stand up while shampooing. Most Schnoodles actually enjoy a good shampoo and soak.

Dogs are less tolerant of being rinsed. Begin by rinsing at the head, and working your way down his body. Try to avoid getting water inside his ears. After that, wrap your dog in a cotton towel made especially for dogs (some have hoodies) and gently pat dry. When drying, use a pet dryer and turn the setting on low, so as to prevent any burning accidents.

Best Brushes for Your Schnoodle

The most popular brush for your Schnoodle is the pin brush. You can also use the slicker brush, which is great for puppies and Schnoodles that have been clipped.

The slicker brush makes grooming easy. It removes the dead hair and debris on your Schnoodle. Pin brushes are used for fluffing your Schnoodle's hair and also when blow drying. Metal combs have wider teeth on one end and smaller teeth on the other end. These help you to get through any matted areas on your Schnoodle's coat.

By using a dematter, which usually has four or more blades that sit sideways along the handle, you're able to brush through thicker matting. You will be able to do so by using the tip of the teeth first until the matting has been removed from the skin. This all has to be done gently.

How To Groom Your Schnoodle

It's actually very simple, even if you've never groomed a dog before. Every part of your Schnoodle needs to be groomed. This means the neck, head, legs, paws, tail, belly area and doggie armpits.

Remember to alternate the areas of the body that you're grooming. You could start with his tail, then move on to combing his left front leg, his chest and so forth. Keeping grooming sessions short and pain free creates the perfect opportunity for bonding.

Brushing your Schnoodle before going out for a walk will promote great show quality looks and good health. Your Schnoodle will also feel terrific afterwards.

Always comb out your Schnoodle's hair before bathing; otherwise you'll end up with more mats and tangles than ever before. Water and the hair dryer will turn basic tangles into mats that will need to be clipped off.

Trimming Your Schnoodle's Hair

Most owners prefer taking their Schnoodles to a professional groomer for cutting and trimming. Nonetheless, if you want to give this a try, you'll need to invest in a grooming table, an electric clipper with a few different sized blades, scissors for grooming and a few other grooming essentials.

Clipping Essentials

Clipping can be daunting. Because the Schnoodle does not shed, they can look scraggly and messy if not clipped. There are many types of clippers. For the perfect show dog look, use medium-priced clippers that have a variety of blades.

In case you just want to trim and style your Schnoodle, your best choice is the professional-style clippers that have more than one speed and many different blades.

Most clippers come cordless, with the Oster brand being pretty much the favorite. Other favored brands include Wahl, Andis and Conair.

Oster is very much preferred because their blades are universal enough that most other manufacturers make their clippers so that Oster-style blades can fit them.

Blades

Most clippers come with blades, yet some don't. Choosing your blade is like an art and always will depend on your dog's breed and coat type. Most blades are full-tooth blades, yet some are skip-tooth blades. Skip-tooth blades are for stand-up coats like Poodle and Schnoodle coats.

Full-tooth blades are used for smooth coats or drop-coated dogs like the Spaniel-type coats. Snap-on-guide combs are plastic combs that you attach to your electric clippers to provide an even cut. This gives you a precise half-inch or one-inch cut guide.

Scissors

There are many reasons for using scissors, but these need to be used with extreme caution on your Schnoodle. Scissors help even out his coat. Sometimes using scissors is easier than using clippers, because scissors will work best for whiskers or stray hairs. They are also great for touch-ups.

Thinning your Schnoodle's coat or blending one layer of hair with another is best done with thinning scissors. These scissors have rows of skipped teeth that cut only every other hair.

All Schnoodles require a basic grooming regimen that keeps them healthy and clean. Deciding on whether to groom your dog at home or to pay for professional grooming is up to you.

Nail Clippers

Nail care should begin with your puppy's first grooming session. Even if your breeder has done a clip prior to your bringing him home, you should teach your puppy to give you his paw. You should be able to hold your Schnoodle's paw in your hand. Start off by massaging each puppy paw and rewarding your Schnoodle with a puppy treat.

Make a big fuss over each nail so that your Schnoodle puppy will soon enjoy having his paws picked up. By doing this, you're gaining your puppy's trust. Paws are sensitive but need to be checked frequently for injuries.

Nail clippers that are designed especially for dogs can be bought online or at any pet store. Nail files are important for filing your Schnoodle's nails after cutting them. Filing should only be done in one direction. Make sure that your Schnoodle stands on a Rubbermaid mat so that he does not slip when grooming or clipping nails.

The best clippers to use on a Schnoodle puppy will be cat nail clippers. These are made especially for thin, small nails. As your Schnoodle grows older, you'll learn to alternate and use the regular dog nail clipper. These cut thicker adult canine nails.

When buying nail clippers, pick up some styptic powder, which can be used on any bleeding caused from a too-closely clipped nail. It also works as an antiseptic. Try not to nick the quick when cutting your Schnoodle's nails.

Hold your Schnoodle upright in your lap against your chest. Here his back will be toward you. Keep a bowl of his favorite treats nearby and reward him when he's relaxed. Then gently hold one paw in one hand and the nail clipper in the other hand. Make sure that there's no hair at the paw tip by pushing it away from the nail tip.

All your Schnoodle's nails need to be fully exposed so as to prevent any painful accidents. Then, hold a paw and clip off the outer portion at the tip of each nail. Be extremely careful when doing this. It's better to cut too little rather than too much nail. Next, use an emery board to shorten and smoothe your Schnoodle's nails.

You'll notice that after clipping, his nails will have a sharp edge. File from the back to the front of the nail.

Ear Care

After any type of water exposure, dry your Schnoodle's ears. The inside part, under the flaps, cannot dry on their own. They do not have upright ears, so there is not enough circulation.

When your Schnoodle comes in after a long hike, walk or from running out in tall grass, check for ticks, foxtails and seeds from other grasses that may work their way down his inner ear and cause an infection.

If your Schnoodle's ears are inflamed, look reddish brown or carry a black substance, this could be ear mites or an ear infection. A bad odor emanating from the ear could very well indicate that he has an ear infection. Watch for signs of your Schnoodle shaking his head, pawing his ears or holding his head at a strange angle. If he does not let you touch his head area, that could possibly indicate an ear infection.

Schnoodles are prone to certain fungal and yeast infections inside their ears. These could be due to allergies. Contact your veterinarian if you notice any symptoms of an ear infection.

Natural ear cleaners for Schnoodles usually contain witch hazel, yucca, Aloe Vera, tea tree oil, chamomile, rosemary and many other plant-based ingredients. These gently remove your dog's ear wax and promote healing.

Photo Credit: Beth and Eric Krueger of California Schnoodles

Eye Care

Check daily around the eyes for any signs of discharge. If your Schnoodle's eyes appear to be cloudy or red or show signs of discharge, contact your veterinarian for a complete examination.

Healthy Schnoodle eyes are bright and have a glow to them. They will have a natural dull pink mucous membrane.

Some Schnoodles also have a droopy lower eyelid. This will allow for gunk to collect, causing an inflammation in your dog's eye. Bathe the area around your dog's eyes daily with a moistened cotton ball.

Symptoms of Gingivitis

This can start as early as two years of age. The inflammation begins on the gums where they meet the teeth. Because food and bacteria now can get stuck in these pockets and cause painful periodontal disease, your Schnoodle may start having tooth loss. If your Schnoodle is suffering from gingivitis, brush his teeth every day so that you're able to massage his gums and encourage healthy healing.

You're still going to have to visit your veterinarian to clean his teeth and to give him a full check-up. This is done under full anesthesia, where your Schnoodle won't feel a thing and won't have to endure any pain.

Your veterinarian will scale and polish his teeth, as well as clean below the gum line, where daily brushing does not reach. Sometimes an extraction or two may be performed alongside a routine mouth examination.

Try purchasing healthy food treats and teeth – cleaning treats that are specially formulated for canine dental care.

Brushing Your Schnoodle's Teeth

Your Schnoodle needs to have his teeth cleaned regularly, followed up with a specialized dental cleaning from his veterinarian once a year. Examine your dog's teeth daily for any bits of food or items that may be lodged between his teeth.

Dogs are not able to clean their teeth by themselves, so in order to prevent plaque, dental buildup and gum disease, it's critical that pet parents pay special attention to their dog's teeth, starting from puppyhood.

Many Schnoodles will dislike having this done for the first time, so go gently and begin by rubbing your dog's gums with some canine toothpaste on your finger. Try not to open his jaws too wide, and he'll soon learn to enjoy the feeling and taste.

Start by lifting up his lips and brushing his teeth and most importantly his gum line. Use tiny circular motions, holding his toothbrush at a 45-degree angle. Then, gently open his mouth and target his back teeth using the same brushing motion.

Fleas and Ticks

If you are going to have a dog for a pet, the time will come when you find a flea — or as I like to call them, a "passenger" — on your pet. This is not the dog's fault, nor is it the end of the world. Certainly you want to deal with the problem immediately, but in the short term, the flea is far happier on the dog than it would be on you.

Never treat a puppy of less than 12 weeks of age with a commercial flea product, and be extremely careful of using these items on adult dogs as well. Most of the major brand products contain pyrethrum, which has been responsible for adverse reactions in small dogs to the point of being fatal. Others have recovered but suffered life-long neurological damage.

The very best thing you can do to get rid of fleas is to give your dog a bath in warm water using a standard canine shampoo. Comb the animal's fur with a fine-toothed flea comb. Any live fleas that you collect in the comb will die when you submerge the comb in hot, soapy water.

Wash all of the dog's bedding and any soft materials with which he has come in contact in hot water. Look for any accumulations of "flea dirt," which is actually excreted blood from adult fleas.

Expect to continue washing the bedding and other surfaces daily for at least a week. You are trying to remove any remaining eggs so that no new fleas hatch out.

If you find a tick on your dog, you can remove the blood-sucking parasite by first coating it with a thick layer of petroleum jelly. Leave this on for up to 5 minutes. The jelly clogs the spiracles through which the tick breathes and causes its jaws to release. You can then simply pluck the tick off with a pair of tweezers with a straight motion. Never just jerk a tick off a dog. The head of the creature will be left behind and will continue to burrow into the skin, making a painful sore.

Photo Credit: Dylan from Kim Cochrane

Chapter 5 - Training Your Schnoodle

Training starts from the minute you bring your Schnoodle home. You may not realize it, but everything you do teaches your Schnoodle puppy how to act. Many dog owners make the mistake of giving their puppy free reign for the first few weeks, and then they are surprised when it comes time for training and the puppy has already developed hard-to-break habits.

A new Schnoodle puppy is very much like a blank slate where you can impress accepted puppy behaviors.

Photo Credit: Sabrina Alstat of Sabrinas Labradoodles

Schnoodles are family dogs that belong with your family. I'd like to recommend positive training with a professional certified trainer. Schnoodle pups are cute, but they do require time and effort, more so than an adult dog. Be prepared to make that commitment.

Dog Whispering or Dog Training?

Many people can be confused when they need professional help with their dog, because for many years, if you needed help with your dog, you contacted a "dog trainer" or took your dog to "puppy classes" where your dog would learn how to sit or stay.

The difference between a dog trainer and a dog whisperer would be that a "dog trainer" teaches a dog how to perform certain tasks, and a "dog whisperer" alleviates behavior problems by teaching humans what they need to do to keep their particular dog happy.

Often, depending on how soon the guardian has sought help, this can mean that the dog in question has developed some pretty serious issues, such as aggressive barking, lunging, biting or attacking other dogs, pets or people.

Dog whispering is often an emotional roller coaster ride for the humans involved that unveils many truths when they finally realize that it has been their actions (or inactions) that have likely caused the unbalanced behavior that their dog is now displaying.

Once solutions are provided, the relief for both dog and human can be quite cathartic when they realize that with the correct direction, they can indeed live a happy life with their dog.

All specific methods of training, such as "clicker training," fall outside of what every dog needs to be happy, because training your dog to respond to a clicker, which you can easily do on your own, and then letting them sleep in your bed, eat from your plate and any other multitude of things humans allow, are what makes the dog unbalanced and causes behavior problems.

I always say to people, don't wait until you have a severe problem before getting some dog whispering or professional help of some sort, because "With the proper training, Man can learn to be dog's best friend."

Positive Training

Schnoodles are half Schnauzer and half Poodle. Both of these breeds are well known for being very intelligent and having an ability to learn quickly. So training your Schnoodle should be an easy process. I find them to be movement-motivated rather than treat-motivated. They love participating in agility and learning plenty of new tricks.

Some Schnoodles may be quite stubborn and dominant. This results from the Schnauzer breed being dominant. With that said, it's important for obedience training to start from an early age, most especially for the larger Schnoodles.

Teaching your puppy the basics in training will allow for him to have the necessary building blocks for becoming a well-adjusted, sociable and obedient family member. You'll be able to take him everywhere and invite friends over to your home without being embarrassed about your puppy's bad behavior.

Start off with short training sessions so that your puppy will focus. Use only positive training methods.

The main objective here is to teach your new puppy what you want him to do and reward him for doing it. There is no punishment involved. After you've taught your puppy what you want, he'll spend his time focusing on the good behaviors and waiting for those healthy treats. It's simple and easy, and is the only form of training that is favored today. Be kind and gentle at all times, even when your puppy is having a hard time and just wants to play around.

All pet parents want a well-behaved, content and stress-free puppy, so with this punishment-free technique your Schnoodle will always be willing to learn.

Positive reinforcement means having consistency in training; practicing every day for a few minutes; and prevention of undesirable Schnoodle puppy behaviors. Positive reinforcement is recommended whenever your puppy does something correctly by rewarding your puppy with his favorite high protein treats and praise.

What Are Verbal Corrections?

Verbal corrections should always be used to encourage, yet they should be given in a firm tone. "No" is an important word in puppy training and should be used to prevent your Schnoodle puppy from doing something dangerous like running in front of a car or chasing a cat.

Give the command verbally when the undesired action is taking place so that your Schnoodle puppy understands what is required from him and when. Adding the word "No" to the undesired behavior makes it easily understood. You may be firm, but need to always be in control.

Verbal corrections should always be given while the undesired puppy behavior is taking place. If you correct your puppy after he has done something incorrectly, it will not help him learn anything and you will only confuse him.

Come

This is the most important command and can be used during an emergency situation as well. The best way to use this command is by teaching it in conjunction with your puppy's name.

• The first step is teaching your Schnoodle puppy his name and to come to you when you call out his name. No matter how long his registered name is, your Schnoodle puppy should have a short name that is easily understood. This is the name that he will respond to when you call him to your side.

• Start by using this name from the day one when he comes home, and use it with the same tone and in the same way every day. If you change names, you'll only end up confusing your Schnoodle, since he won't know that you're calling him.

• Never call him to you unless you know that he's focused. Never use the word "come" and not expect your Schnoodle to pay attention to you.

• Place a collar on your puppy (that's only after he's gone through the collar familiarization process), then attach his leash to it. Refer to Step 2.

Step One

• Use your Schnoodle puppy's name correctly, and call him over to you when he's awake and looking at you. You may also clap your hands gently to get his attention.

• Repeat this a few times, making a huge fuss about what a great Schnoodle puppy he is and rewarding him with his favorite tidbit when he responds.

• This will teach him to come to you when he hears you call out his name. He will understand that he's being called, and when he does respond, he'll be warmly greeted and rewarded with his favorite treat.

Step Two

• When your Schnoodle puppy has had a few days to get used to you, you can now put on a light puppy collar, so that he can become used to having it on around his neck. In the beginning, your Schnoodle puppy may make a huge fuss, rolling around on the ground, struggling or trying to paw it off his neck. Reward with a small treat and try to distract him.

• Have a tasty tidbit on hand so that you can get him to focus his attention on you and the treat, then play with him. In a short time, he will no longer want to remove the lightweight collar. Remove the collar after a few minutes.

Step Three

• The very next step in puppy training your puppy is to have him become used to the lightweight leash. Use a lightweight leash and attach it to your puppy's collar.

• Carry your puppy outdoors where there will be a few things that will distract him. Allow for your Schnoodle to investigate everything after placing him down. At this stage, your Schnoodle may not yet feel the leash dangling behind him, or he may make a huge fuss about it.

• If he does fuss, repeat the diversion and show him something of interest, perhaps a puppy bone or ball. When he does eventually accept the leash, hold the end part of it and follow him around.

• Many puppies will start struggling and pulling against the leash and try to slip out of the collar and leash. They may possibly also bite at it. Pat your Schnoodle and reward him each time he accepts the leash. Try this for a few minutes each time several times a day.

Photo Credit: Dizzy from Louise Dohm

Step Four

• When your Schnoodle puppy no longer pulls against the leash, try to direct him in the direction you want to go. Never pull on the leash, as this will frighten him or possibly hurt him, and he may start resenting his leash. As he grows into adolescence and becomes stronger and possibly more stubborn, there may very well be a battle of the wills, where both of you will be pulling in opposite directions. This is why it's so important to begin with basic training from a young age.

• The most favorable method is a gentle pull in your direction. Keep up with the encouragement and reward him each time he gets started. Repeat the word "come" throughout the complete duration of puppy training.

• Once your Schnoodle puppy has mastered this step and starts walking easily on his leash, the next step is to show him how to follow you on your left side only. If you use this method consistently, your Schnoodle puppy will come to you each and every time.

Step Five

• With this new step, you need to use the same method as you used previously when teaching your Schnoodle puppy how to respond to you while on his leash. This time you use the word "heel."

• This is not done in one day or even a few days. Your Schnoodle puppy will learn this over a period of a few weeks. All the while, puppy training is done slowly and with plenty of encouragement, praise and treats. You need to make your Schnoodle puppy understand that positive training is fun. The amount of time that it takes for this step to be completed will depend on your puppy, his personality and aptitude. Keep in mind that all Schnoodles become excited with their training and are keen learners.

• This is a great method of training. You're teaching your furry best friend to be a problem solver, and you're teaching him that you've got something that he wants and asking him what he should do to get it right away. After a short time, your pup will know. This form of training is fun for everyone.

• This method works well for puppies that are fearful, aggressive or hard to train. Many puppies that don't enjoy being touched respond best to this method of training.

• In the beginning, it may take longer, yet once your furry companion knows how to get his treat, puppy training works quickly. With this form of training, you can teach your Schnoodle puppy to do anything, including fun tricks.

• Start off by waiting for your Schnoodle puppy to offer you the behavior that you want. When the behavior occurs, reward with a food treat or clicker sound immediately.

Lure/Reward Training

Sit

• By luring your Schnoodle puppy to move his nose, his entire body will follow. Luring is done by holding a treat in your hand and lifting it upwards and backwards over your puppy's nose. When this is done, his hindquarters will go down into a natural sitting position almost immediately, as he looks upwards at the treat. The sit command is the easiest of all to teach.

• End this with a "click" from the clicker or "Good Boy" and his favorite treat. The marker indicates that the behavior is now completed. When your Schnoodle puppy is ready to follow your hand movement into the "sit" position, you can always predict when your Schnoodle puppy will sit down. With that said, say "sit" before you move the lure-treat, and click when his rear end touches the ground. Reward and praise.

Physical Prompting

• With puppy training, you can use physical prompting to make your Schnoodle puppy follow simple commands like sit, lie down, stay or stand. If the prompt is done in the right way, your puppy will learn that if he's touched on his rump or between the shoulders that he should take up the proper position. This form of training was popular in the 80s, yet is no longer popular today because it's very time consuming and hard work for everyone, most especially your furry best friend.

• Instead, teach your Schnoodle puppy some verbal commands from the beginning by familiarizing your puppy to capturing and shaping, or luring/reward training. This tends to be easier for all puppies and adult dogs.

• Training your Schnoodle to follow simple commands like come, sit, down and stay down is probably one of the most important safety measures you can take for both you and your furry best friend. Since Schnoodle puppies are fun to train, this should take you no time at all.

Sit/Stay

When your Schnoodle understands the sit command properly, you can start teaching him the sit/stay command. After your Schnoodle puppy sits, you then will give him the stay command. In the beginning, your puppy will not understand this new command and will make every attempt to get up.

• Gently repeat "sit" and "stay" commands. When he does this and remains seated for a few seconds, reward and praise him.

• Continue asking your puppy to sit, adding the stay command. Your Schnoodle puppy should be able to do this for a few seconds after a few repetitions for several days.

• Reward and praise each correct behavior.

• As he begins to understand and do the required behavior, you may increase the amount of time that your Schnoodle puppy remains seated.

• This command is important when you're working off leash.

• Keeping your Schnoodle safe is important. After he's learned all the basic commands, you'll find it much easier to control him.

Schnoodles cannot exhibit many bad behaviors at the same time. If your puppy is jumping up on your children, or sprinting out of the front door, you can use the sit command. This will stop him from jumping up on your guests.

Photo Credit: Toby from Nancy Simmons

Down

• Move the treat forwards away from your Schnoodle puppy and then down; in this way, your puppy will follow the treat with his nose. As he begins to lie down, give him the command "Down." Reward and praise him immediately. If, on the other hand, your Schnoodle refuses to lie down, gently lift up his front legs into a begging position, and then gently lower it down, rewarding your furry best friend for his attempts.

• While you're still gently holding the collar, continue moving his food treat forward and down until your pup is lying down completely on the ground. Reward with the treat and praise. Don't praise too much, or your puppy will become way too excited and start jumping up on you. You may repeat this a few times following each repetition with your Schnoodle's favorite treat.

Down/Stay Command

• This is great for teaching your Schnoodle puppy to wait until it's his turn to do something.

• Try this when he's tired – this will make training for this cue much easier.

• The down command is sometimes followed by the "Stay" command, which will last for a few seconds and will gradually work up to a few minutes. This is a good command for all dogs to learn. This is an effective way to teach your Schnoodle to remain "down" during grooming sessions or when guests come to visit you.

• Follow the "down" command cues and only when your Schnoodle puppy is comfortable with this, add the "stay" cue.

When your puppy is comfortable with you going away from him, try moving to his side, one step at a time to begin with. Reward. Next, move behind him and so forth. Keep rewarding with tasty bits of food.

Loose Leash Walking

There are so many dogs that don't know how to walk on a leash. You'll see pet parents being walked by their dogs. It's actually very easy to correct.

Proper leash training should start from the very first day when taking your Schnoodle out for a walk. Your puppy needs to understand that he needs to stay right next to your side. Walking your Schnoodle will become an important part of your life. You'll develop a special bond with your dog.

• When you've taught your Schnoodle how to walk calmly next to you, you'll then need to teach him how not to pull on his leash. This will make walking him so much more pleasant.

• Leashes should be kept loose most of the time to make walking your Schnoodle puppy more enjoyable.

• Stop walking the very minute he pulls at his leash.

• If your Schnoodle is strong and pulls frantically, hold the leash toward your middle.

• Stop and wait. Do not let your puppy go any further. You'll need to teach him that when his leash goes tight and he pulls, the walking stops immediately.

• Bring him back to you and start walking again. Repeat this every time he pulls. He'll soon learn not to pull during his walks.

• Be consistent with training. When your Schnoodle puppy understands what you want and follows you calmly, relax the leash.

Retrieving Tips

A fun game of fetch is usually a requirement for Schnoodles. This breed is energetic and also has a lot of fun playing in water. You can even extend retrieving exercises to the swimming pool or ocean.

Schnoodles are known for being able to race as fast as they can. Some breeders call this the "Schnoodle 500." In this game, Schnoodles tuck in their hindquarters and race around as fast as they can. They will do this around, over and inside of everything that they come across. It's usually in a circular pattern. Schnoodles are not running from anything when they do this. It's actually a sudden burst of Schnoodle energy and will only last a few short minutes.

• Retrieving teaches him how to fetch a ball and bring it back.

• It helps him to get rid of excess energy while having fun. Don't allow for your Schnoodle to become a couch potato.

• Before throwing the ball, get your puppy excited. Move the ball erratically up and down so that he wants to play the game.

• Next, throw the ball a short distance away from you. As soon as your Schnoodle retrieves the ball, encourage him to come back to you either by calling his name or patting your thighs while crouching close to the ground.

• Praise without taking the ball out of his mouth.

• When your Schnoodle puppy knows how to retrieve, you can teach him to drop the ball right in front of you. If he's bored with this, try rolling the ball gently with your hand.

• When your Schnoodle puppy has the ball in his mouth, lower your hand directly under his mouth and get ready to catch the ball.

• Reward and praise.

Having a well-trained Schnoodle is similar to having a well-behaved child. All dog breeds can be trained and can be asked to learn many things. Never leave your Schnoodle at home to his own devices. Arrange for a pet sitter to come by and take him out for walks if you need to spend your day at work.

Marking Territory

Both intact male and female dogs will mark territory by urinating. This is most often an outdoor behavior but can happen inside if a new dog is introduced to the household.

Again, use an enzymatic cleaner to remove the odor so the dog will not be attracted to use the same spot again. Since this behavior is most often seen in intact males displaying dominance, the obvious solution is to have the dog neutered.

If this is not possible, and the behavior continues, it may be necessary to separate the animals or to work with a trainer to resolve dominance issues in your little "pack."

Marking territory is not a consequence of poor housetraining, and the behavior can be seen in dogs that would otherwise never go in the house. If you are consistent in taking your puppy outside frequently and in rewarding him for good behavior (doing his business in the designated area), you should have no trouble at all with housetraining.

Rewarding Unwanted Behavior

It is very important to recognize that any attention paid to an out-of-control, adolescent puppy, even negative attention, is likely to be exciting and rewarding for your Schnoodle puppy.

Chasing after a puppy when they have taken something they shouldn't have, picking them up when barking or showing aggression, pushing them off when they jump on other people, or yelling when they refuse to come when called are all forms of attention that can actually be rewarding for most puppies.

It will be your responsibility to provide structure for your puppy, which will include finding acceptable and safe ways to allow your puppy to vent their energy without being destructive or harmful to others.

The worst thing you can do when training your Schnoodle is to yell at him or use punishment. Positive reinforcement training methods – that is, rewarding your dog for good behavior – are infinitely more effective than negative reinforcement – training by punishment.

It is important when training your Schnoodle that you do not allow yourself to get frustrated. If you feel yourself starting to get angry, take a break and come back to the training session later.

Why is punishment-based training so bad? Think about it this way – your dog should listen to you because he wants to please you, right?

If you train your dog using punishment, he could become fearful of you and that could put a damper on your relationship with him. Do your dog and yourself a favor by using positive reinforcement.

Beyond Basic Training

Once your Schnoodle has a firm grasp on the basics, you can move on to teaching him additional commands. You can also add distractions to the equation to reinforce your dog's mastery of the commands. The end goal is to ensure that your Schnoodle responds to your command each and every time – regardless of distractions and anything else he might rather be doing. This is incredibly important, because there may come a time when your dog is in a dangerous situation and if he doesn't respond to your command, he could get hurt.

Photo Credit: Beth and Eric Krueger of California Schnoodles

Reinforcing Your Schnoodle's Response

After your Schnoodle has started to respond correctly to the basic commands on a regular basis, you can start to incorporate distractions.

If you previously conducted your training sessions indoors, you might consider moving them outside where your dog could be distracted by various sights, smells and sounds.

One thing you might try is to give your dog the Stay command and then toss a toy nearby that will tempt him to break his Stay. Start by tossing the toy at a good distance from him and wait a few seconds before you release him to play.

Eventually, you will be able to toss a toy right next to your dog without him breaking his Stay until you give him permission to do so.

Incorporating Hand Signals

Teaching your Schnoodle to respond to hand signals in addition to verbal commands is very useful – you never know when you will be in a situation where your dog might not be able to hear you.

To start out, choose your dominant hand to give the hand signals, and hold a small treat in that hand while you are training your dog – this will encourage your dog to focus on your hand during training, and it will help to cement the connection between the command and the hand signal.

To begin, give your dog the Sit or Down command while holding the treat in your dominant hand, and give the appropriate hand signal – for Sit you might try a closed fist and, for Down, you might place your hand flat, parallel to the ground.

When your dog responds correctly, give him the treat. You will need to repeat this process many times in order for your dog to form a connection between both the verbal command and the hand signal with the desired behavior.

Eventually, you can start to remove the verbal command from the equation – use the hand gesture every time, but start to use the verbal command only half the time.

Once your dog gets the hang of this, you should start to remove the food reward from the equation. Continue to give your dog the hand signal for each command, and occasionally use the verbal command just to remind him.

You should start to phase out the food rewards, however, by offering them only half the time. Progressively lessen the use of the food reward, but continue to praise your dog for performing the behavior correctly so he learns to repeat it.

First Tricks

Training your Schnoodle for tricks is an easy way to practice obedience skills for both you and your Schnoodle. Teaching your dog how to do simple tricks builds his self-confidence. If you are wanting to participate in animal-assisted therapy, you can teach your Schnoodle to do a variety of tricks that can be developed into a routine to entertain sick children at hospitals. He could even get cast in a movie. Start by working with the behaviors that come naturally to your Schnoodle, and use plenty of praise and treats each time he gets the trick right. Here are some fun tips on how to train for tricks:

• Work on your Schnoodle's natural behaviors.

• Train only for a few minutes at a time, keeping the activity fun and rewarding for your dog.

• Reward with his favorite treat – hot dog bits, cheese, hamburger bits or baby carrots.

• As with any form of training, use patience, kindness and respect with your Schnoodle at all times.

• Each training session should end on a positive note with your Schnoodle's favorite treat.

Shake a Paw

Who doesn't love a dog who knows how to shake a paw? This is one of the easiest tricks to teach your Schnoodle.

TIP: Most dogs are naturally either right or left pawed. If you know which paw your dog favors, ask them to shake this paw.

Find a quiet place to practice, without noisy distractions or other pets, and stand or sit in front of your dog. Place them in the sitting position and hold a treat in your left hand.

Say the command "Shake" while putting your right hand behind their left or right paw and pulling the paw gently toward yourself until you are holding their paw in your hand. Immediately praise them and give them the treat.

Most dogs will learn the "Shake" trick very quickly, and in no time at all, once you put out your hand, your Schnoodle will immediately lift their paw and put it into your hand, without your assistance or any verbal cue.

Practice every day until they are 100% reliable with this trick, and then it will be time to add another trick to their repertoire.

Roll Over

You will find that just like your Schnoodle is naturally either right or left pawed, they will also naturally want to roll either to the right or the left side. Take advantage of this by asking your dog to roll to the side they naturally prefer.

Sit with your dog on the floor and put them in a lie down position. Hold a treat in your hand and place it close to their nose without allowing them to grab it, and while they are in the lying position, move the treat to the right or left side of their head so that they have to roll over to get to it.

Photo Credit: Midge from Dena Holmes

You will quickly see which side they want to naturally roll to; once you see this, move the treat to that side. Once they roll over to that side, immediately give them the treat and praise them.

You can say the verbal cue "Over" while you demonstrate the hand signal motion (moving your right hand in a half circular motion) from one side of their head to the other.

Sit Pretty

While this trick is a little more complicated, and most dogs pick up on it very quickly, remember that this trick requires balance, and every dog is different, so always exercise patience.

Find a quiet space with few distractions, and sit or stand in front of your dog and ask them to "Sit."

Have a treat nearby (on a countertop or table) and when they sit, use both of your hands to lift up their front paws into the sitting pretty position, while saying the command "Sit Pretty." Help them balance in this position while you praise them and give them the treat.

Once your Schnoodle can do the balancing part of the trick quite easily without your help, sit or stand in front of your dog while asking them to "Sit Pretty" and hold the treat above their head, at the level their nose would be when they sit pretty.

If they attempt to stand on their back legs to get the treat, you may be holding the treat too high, which will encourage them to stand up on their back legs to reach it. Go back to the first step and put them back into the "Sit" position and again lift their paws while their backside remains on the floor.

The hand signal for "Sit Pretty" is a straight arm held over your dog's head with a closed fist.

TIP: Place your Schnoodle beside a wall when first teaching this trick so that they can use the wall to help their balance.

A young Schnoodle puppy should be able to easily learn these basic tricks before they are six months old, and when you are patient and make your training sessions short and fun for your dog, they will be eager to learn more.

Dealing With Problem Behaviors

Most behaviors that dog owners identify as problems are actually behaviors that are completely natural for dogs. It is natural for your dog to dig, to bark and to chew on things – it only becomes a problem when that behavior is exhibited in a destructive way. The best way to deal with these problems, then, is not to try to eradicate them entirely but to redirect them to a more appropriate outlet.

Barking

For the most part, Schnoodles are not yappy breeds, but if your dog learns that barking gets him the attention he wants, he may be more likely to do it.

For example, if your Schnoodle has a tendency to bark when the doorbell rings and then whoever comes through the door rewards him by petting him, he will only learn to repeat that behavior.

The first step to teaching your Schnoodle not to bark is to teach him to bark on command – then you can teach him a command to stop barking.

To do so, you will need the help of a friend or family member. Have that person stand outside your door, ready to ring the doorbell.

Give your Schnoodle a "Speak" command and have your friend immediately ring the doorbell to get your dog to bark. When he does, reward him with praise and a treat. After a few barks, give your dog the "Hush" or "Quiet" command and reward him when he stops barking.

If your dog doesn't immediately stop barking, try waving the treat in front of his nose to catch his attention.

Chewing

If you do not give your Schnoodle enough exercise or attention, he may develop a problem with destructive chewing.

In some cases, chewing behavior develops as a symptom of separation anxiety – your dog may become nervous about being left alone and resorts to chewing as a way to work out his anxiety. In most cases, however, chewing is simply a behavior that dogs develop because they are bored.

The key to dealing with chewing behavior is to redirect it to a more appropriate outlet. Make sure your dog has plenty of chew toys to choose from – try using a variety of toys, including Kong toys that you can fill with treats like peanut butter.

When you catch your Schnoodle chewing on something he shouldn't be, take the item away while saying "No" in a firm voice. Immediately give your dog one of his toys and praise him when he begins to chew on it instead. Eventually, your dog will learn what he is and is not allowed to chew on.

The Canine Good Citizen Test

Otherwise known as the CGC certification program, the Canine Good Citizen Test stresses the importance of good manners in dogs, as well as the importance of good canine management on the part of pet parents. Any dog, regardless of whether they belong to the American Kennel Club (AKC) or whether they're a hybrid or purebred, can participate and earn the CGC.

Today, there are many apartment complexes or Home Owners Associations that require this test before dog owners can get approved into the unit or home. This test can be done at most dog clubs and achieves the following:

- Accepting a stranger approaching
- Sitting quietly while being petted
- Grooming and appearance petiquette
- Walking on a loose leash
- Walking through a crowded place
- Sit, down and stay commands down pat
- Come on command
- Dog must react politely when approached by another pooch
- Respectful behavior and reaction to distraction

Photo Credit: Tess & Cooper from Sandy Ross

Chapter 6 - Keeping Your Schnoodle Healthy

Your dog is more than just a pet – he is a member of the family and quite possibly your best friend. This being the case, you want to take care of him as much as possible.

Unfortunately, you can't keep your Schnoodle in a bubble where he will never be exposed to disease. You can, however, learn as much as you can about the diseases to which he might be exposed so you know how to handle them. The sooner you start treatment for a disease or condition, the greater your Schnoodle's chances of recovery are.

Photo Credit: Molly from Kevin & Juli-Ann Hills

Working With Your Veterinarian

If you do not already have a veterinarian with whom you work, finding a qualified doctor is the first step in ensuring your dog's long-term good health. Ask your breeder for a recommendation, or if you have worked with a kennel outside of your immediate area, try to connect with other Schnoodle owners in your locale.

Make an appointment to go into the clinic to see the facility and meet the vet. Be clear that you are there to discuss becoming a client and will happily pay the fee for a visit. Prepare your questions in advance so you don't waste anyone's time — including your own. Some questions you will want answered include:

• How long has your clinic been open?
• What hours do you operate?
• What medical services do you offer?
• What grooming services do you offer?
• Do you have an estimated schedule of fees?
• How many vets are on staff?
• Do you provide emergency services after hours?
• Are there any specialists in your practice?
• Where do you refer dogs in need of a specialist?
• Do you currently treat any Schnoodles?

Pay attention to how you are greeted when you arrive at the clinic. Does the staff seem friendly and approachable? Are they well organized? Is there a bulletin board in the waiting room with notes and photos from patients? That's always a good sign of a satisfied clientele. Does the facility seem modern and up-to-date? Is it clean, airy and light? Are the doctor's credentials prominently displayed?

Hybrid Genetic Concerns

Hybrids are generally healthy, and do not have as many genetic or inherited problems as purebred dogs. Hybrid vigor, also known as outbreeding enhancement and "heterosis," creates stronger characteristics in hybrid dogs like Schnoodles.

Today, Schnoodle breeders are making sure that they breed a healthier hybrid dog by combining the virtues of both parents. Nonetheless, not all hybrid dogs are healthier and live longer. Often, certain mixed breeds produce inferior offspring whereby the puppies have inherited traits that do not make them fit for survival.

Schnoodles have not been bred for as long as some other crossbreeds; yet there are indications that the Schnoodle is healthy, intelligent and good looking.

Vaccinations

By the time you've arrived home with your new Schnoodle puppy around 8 weeks of age, your Schnoodle will have already received one or two of the series of puppy immunizations. These will protect him from dangerous diseases such as parvovirus, parainfluenza, distemper and canine hepatitis.

These vaccines will be the beginning of a series of vaccinations. All these vaccinations are necessary to keep your Schnoodle healthy. The usual vaccine protocol will be 6 weeks, 8 weeks, 10 weeks, 12 weeks and 16 weeks.

Puppies are all protected by the antibodies in their mother's milk. This protection gradually declines, and your Schnoodle puppy will then start to produce his own antibodies. Core vaccines will protect your Schnoodle puppy from catching diseases.

What Is a Puppy Vaccine?

The process of giving a puppy shot to a dog is called a vaccination. All puppy vaccines have substances called antigens. These stimulate a response in your puppy's immune system, protecting him against any possible future exposure to a specific disease.

Puppies and dogs will receive vaccines that protect against viral hepatitis, adenovirus, leptospirosis, parainfluenza, parvovirus, rabies and coronavirus. Puppies used to receive a single combination puppy shot called the DHLPPC or DALPPC.

Many dog owners and veterinarians alike believe that too many vaccinations or puppy shots are harmful and possibly dangerous to dogs because they can overload the immune system. Instead, many dog owners are spacing out the vaccinations, deliberately giving only one or two at a time.

It's important to know that even if your Schnoodle puppy has been given his puppy vaccinations, he can still become sick. Puppy vaccines are not 100% effective. This will happen for many reasons. Some puppies don't have a strong immune system that functions properly. Nutrition, stress, anxiety and many other environmental factors may interfere with puppy immunity.

Distemper

Canine distemper is a contagious and serious viral illness for which there is currently no known cure.

This deadly virus, which is spread either through the air or by direct or indirect contact with a dog that is already infected or other distemper-carrying wildlife, including ferrets, raccoons, foxes, skunks and wolves, is a relative of the measles virus that affects humans.

Canine distemper is sometimes also called "hard pad disease," because some strains of the distemper virus actually cause thickening of the pads on a dog's feet, which can also affect the end of a dog's nose.

Early symptoms of distemper include fever, loss of appetite and mild eye inflammation that may only last a day or two. Symptoms become more serious and noticeable as the disease progresses. In dogs or animals with weak immune systems, death may result two to five weeks after the initial infection.

A puppy or dog that survives the distemper virus will usually continue to experience symptoms or signs of the disease throughout their remaining lifespan, including "hard pad disease" as well as "enamel hypoplasia," which is damage to the enamel of the puppy's teeth that are not yet formed or that have not yet pushed through the gums. Enamel hypoplasia is caused by the distemper virus killing the cells that manufacture tooth enamel.

Adenovirus

This virus causes infectious canine hepatitis, which can range in severity from very mild to very serious, or even cause death.

Symptoms can include coughing, loss of appetite, increased thirst and urination, tiredness, runny eyes and nose, vomiting, bruising or bleeding under the skin, swelling of the head, neck and trunk, fluid accumulation in the abdomen area, jaundice (yellow tinge to the skin), a bluish clouding of the cornea of the eye (called "hepatitis blue eye") and seizures.

There is no specific treatment for infectious canine hepatitis, and treatment is focused on managing symptoms while the virus runs its course. Hospitalization and intravenous fluid therapy may be required in severe cases.

Photo Credit: Renee Sweeley of Pierce Schnoodles

Parainfluenza Virus

The canine parainfluenza virus originally affected only horses but has now adapted to become contagious to dogs. Also referred to as "canine influenza virus," "greyhound disease" or "race flu," it is easily spread from dog to dog through the air or by coming into contact with respiratory secretions from an infected animal.

While the more frequent occurrences of this respiratory infection are seen in areas with high dog populations, such as race tracks, boarding kennels and pet stores, this virus is highly contagious to any dog or puppy, regardless of age.

Symptoms can include a dry, hacking cough, difficulty breathing, wheezing, runny nose and eyes, sneezing, fever, loss of appetite, tiredness, depression and possible pneumonia.

In cases where only a cough exists, tests will be required to determine whether the cause of the cough is the parainfluenza virus or the less serious "kennel cough."

While many dogs can naturally recover from this virus, they will remain contagious. For this reason, to prevent the spread to other animals, aggressive treatment of the virus with antibiotics and antiviral drugs will be the prescribed course of action.

In more severe cases, a cough suppressant may be used, as well as intravenous fluids to prevent secondary bacterial infection.

Parvovirus

Canine parvovirus is a highly contagious viral illness affecting puppies and dogs that also affects other canine species, including foxes, coyotes and wolves.

There are two forms of this virus — (1) the more common intestinal form and (2) the less common cardiac form, which can cause death in young puppies.

Symptoms of the intestinal form of parvovirus include vomiting, bloody diarrhea, weight loss and lack of appetite, while the less common cardiac form attacks the heart muscle.

Early vaccination in young puppies has radically reduced the incidence of canine parvovirus infection, which is easily transmitted either by direct contact with an infected dog or indirectly, by sniffing an infected dog's feces.

The virus can also be brought into a dog's environment on the bottom of human shoes that may have stepped on infected feces, and this hardy virus can live in ground soil for up to a year.

Recovery from parvovirus requires both aggressive and early treatment. With proper treatment, death rates are relatively low (between 5 and 20%), although the chances of survival for puppies are much lower than older dogs, and in all instances, there is no guarantee of survival.

Treatment of parvovirus requires hospitalization where intravenous fluids and nutrients are administered to help combat dehydration. As well, antibiotics will be given to counteract secondary bacterial infections, and as necessary, medications to control nausea and vomiting may be given.

Without prompt and proper treatment, dogs that have severe parvovirus infections can die within 48 to 72 hours.

Rabies Vaccinations

Rabies is a viral disease transmitted through the saliva of an infected animal, usually through a bite. The virus travels to the brain along the nerves, and once symptoms develop, death is almost certainly inevitable, usually following a prolonged period of suffering.

I highly recommend that the rabies vaccine be given separately, by at least a few days, from all other vaccines. I know of several Schnoodles who had reactions to the combined vaccines.

Most countries require a rabies vaccination and rabies certificate. If you're going to be taking your Schnoodle to puppy training classes, you'll need to provide valid proof of this vaccine. Some dogs may produce antithyroglobulin autoantibodies after being vaccinated with the rabies vaccine. This sometimes causes the development of hypothyroidism later on in life.

Leishmaniasis

Leishmaniasis is caused by a parasite and is transmitted by a bite from a sand fly. There is no definitive answer for effectively combating leishmaniasis, especially since one vaccine will not prevent the known multiple species.

Note: Leishmaniasis is a "zoonotic" infection, which means that this is a contagious disease, and that organisms residing in the Leishmaniasis lesions can be spread between animals and humans and, ultimately, transmitted to humans.

Lyme Disease

This is one of the most common tick-borne diseases in the world, which is transmitted by Borrelia bacteria found in the deer or sheep tick. Lyme disease, also called "borreliosis," can affect both humans and dogs, and can be fatal.

There is a vaccine for Lyme disease, and dogs living in areas that have easy access to these ticks should be vaccinated yearly.

Worming

Your Schnoodle puppy will need to be wormed at two, four, six and eight weeks of age for roundworms. If your breeder has used a worming program and your puppy is free of worms, it's still in the Schnoodle's best interests to keep up with deworming.

Many worms are easily transmitted from the mother dog to her puppies. If the Schnoodle mother dog had roundworms, even during puppyhood, the beginning stages of these worms will lie dormant in the Schnoodle mother dog. When she becomes pregnant, there are certain hormones that are excreted into her system. It is during this stage that the worms become energized and start traveling in her bloodstream. They then migrate to the puppies via the umbilical cord.

Many puppies are born with worms in their system. Always remember to ask your Schnoodle breeder for a veterinary health certificate. Make sure that you bring home a healthy Schnoodle puppy rather than a sickly one who may have permanent damage that will result in huge veterinary bills.

Common Health Issues in Schnoodles

Cardiomyopathy

This is one of the most common heart conditions in dogs. This disease causes the heart muscle of the dog to become inflamed, which impairs its function. There are two different types of cardiomyopathy – dilated cardiomyopathy and hypertrophic cardiomyopathy.

In cases of dilated cardiomyopathy (DCM), the chambers of the heart increase in size (dilate), which stretches the muscles thin – this is one of the leading causes of heart failure in dogs. Hypertrophic cardiomyopathy involves thickening of the heart chamber walls, which leads to decreased pumping efficiency.

The causes of cardiomyopathy are unknown, though some breeds have a higher risk than others, depending on various factors like low blood potassium levels, toxic injury to the heart and low blood supply to the heart.

Symptoms of this condition include shortness of breath, coughing, exercise intolerance, lethargy and loss of appetite. Treatment typically involves controlling the symptoms with medications, because no cure for the disease is available.

Cause: unknown, various factors may increase a dog's risk
Symptoms: shortness of breath, coughing, exercise intolerance, lethargy and loss of appetite
Treatment: medication to control symptoms, no cure

Photo Credit: Tiffany from Peggy Schatzberg

Hip Dysplasia

This is a disease that affects the hip joints of many dog breeds, though small breeds are typically less affected than larger breeds.

Hip dysplasia occurs when the head of the femur pops out of or doesn't rest properly within the hip joint. This results in pain and discomfort in movement, as well as progressive osteoarthritis. If the condition isn't treated, it can result in lameness in the leg.

This condition can be treated either medically or surgically, depending on the severity of the case.

Because hip dysplasia is a hereditary condition, its development cannot be prevented, but the use of anti-inflammatory medications can help decrease its progression.

Surgical corrections for the condition are also possible to correct the problem with the bone and joint.

Cause: congenital (inherited), femur head pops out of the hip joint
Symptoms: pain and discomfort in movement, progressive osteoarthritis, lameness
Treatment: anti-inflammatory medications to manage pain, surgical corrections are often necessary

Legg-Calve Perthes

This is a condition that affects the hip joints and results in the obstruction of blood supply to the femur bone, which then causes the head of the femur itself to deteriorate over time.

This disease typically manifests early, between 4 and 6 months of age, and it may present in the form of a limp or atrophied leg muscle.

The cause of this disease is unknown, and it is possible for it to come on without warning. If the condition isn't treated, it can progress to severe pain, restricted movement, wasting of the thigh muscle and eventual lameness in the affected leg.

When the case is minor, the symptoms can be managed with pain medication and exercise of the femur.

Chapter 6 - Keeping Your Schnoodle Healthy

As the disease progresses, however, surgery may be the only option. With surgery and physical therapy, a 3 to 6 month recovery period can be expected.

Cause: unknown, deterioration of the head of the femur bone
Symptoms: pain, restricted movement, wasting of thigh muscle, lameness in affected leg
Treatment: pain medication and physical therapy, surgical correction may be needed

Lens Luxation

Lens luxation is a hereditary condition characterized by the dislocation of the lens of the eye. Symptoms may include discharge or reddening of the eye, along with an inability or difficulty in opening the eye.

In severe cases, lens luxation can lead to permanent blindness – that is why it is essential that you seek treatment for this condition as early as possible. Some cases can be treated with medication or surgery; it simply depends on the severity of the case. In the event that blindness occurs, however, dogs are generally able to adapt well to the loss of sight.

Cause: congenital (inherited), lens of the eye becomes dislocated
Symptoms: discharge, redness, difficulty opening the eye, loss of vision
Treatment: medication may help but surgery is often needed to repair the problem

Nerve Degeneration

Also referred to as degenerative myelopathy, nerve degeneration is a condition that is fairly common in older dogs – as your

Schnoodle ages, you should keep an eye out for signs of this condition.

Nerve degeneration is a progressive disease that leads to weakness and paralysis in the hindquarters. Over time, the parts of the spinal cord that are responsible for nerve impulses break down, which leads to increased difficulty in muscle control and coordination.

Symptoms of this condition include awkward movement, dragging the feet and eventual inability to walk.

This disease typically affects dogs over the age of 5, and it takes several months to a year to fully set in. Unfortunately, there is no cure for this condition, but the symptoms can be managed through physical therapy.

Cause: degeneration of spinal cord, weakened nerve impulses
Symptoms: awkward movement, dragging the feet and eventual inability to walk
Treatment: no cure, though physical therapy may help with management of symptoms

Patellar Luxation

This condition affects the patella, or kneecap, of the dog, and it is a fairly common condition in many breeds.

Patellar luxation is characterized by the dislocation of the kneecap – it doesn't return to its normal position in the groove of the femur bone as it should.

Symptoms of this condition may vary depending on the severity of the case, but they usually include pain and difficulty moving. In more severe cases, this condition can lead to lameness.

There are two causes for this condition – it can either be inherited or caused by injury to the leg. When the condition is hereditary, it typically manifests by 4 months of age.

In mild cases, medical management of symptoms may be possible, but surgery is generally required to correct the problem and to prevent lameness.

Cause: congenital (inherited) or injury to the leg, involves dislocation of the knee cap
Symptoms: pain, difficulty moving, lameness
Treatment: medication for pain management, surgical correction is often needed

Progressive Retinal Atrophy

This condition is a disease affecting the eye; it is also simply referred to as PRA. Progressive retinal atrophy is an inherited eye disorder.

Though the condition is not painful, it can lead to eventual blindness. During the initial stages of PRA, affected dogs may exhibit dilated pupils and increased eye shine. As it progresses, many dogs develop night blindness. Once PRA progresses to the point where night blindness occurs, it is really only a matter of time before the dog's day vision is affected as well.

Signs of vision loss include difficulty dealing with changes in the home (such as rearranging furniture) and your dog failing to wander as far as he used to on walks and in the yard.

There is no treatment for PRA, but most dogs that develop vision loss are able to adapt well.

Cause: congenital (inherited)

Symptoms: dilated pupils, increased eye shine, night blindness, loss of vision
Treatment: no treatment available

Spaying and Neutering

Spaying or neutering your Schnoodle puppy is typically a requirement of the adoption agreement. These procedures, however, beyond eliminating unwanted pregnancies, also carry significant health benefits for your pet.

Neutered males face a reduced risk of prostatic disease or perianal tumors. The surgery also reduces many aggressive behaviors and lessens the dog's territorial instinct. He will be less likely to mark territory or to behave inappropriately against the legs of your visitors.

Spayed females no longer face the prospect of uterine or ovarian cancer and have a diminished risk for breast cancer. You will not have to deal with your pet coming into season, nor will she experience hormonally related mood swings.

Neutering and spaying surgeries are typically performed around six months of age. The procedures don't make the dogs any more prone to gain weight.

"Normal" Health Issues

Although Schnoodle are, on a whole, happy and healthy, there are some issues that can arise that should be treated by or evaluated by a veterinarian to be on the safe side. Anytime that your dog seems inattentive or lethargic and stops eating or drinking water, seek medical attention for your pet immediately.

Note: Any gastrointestinal upset in dogs can be linked to ingestion of toxic household or garden plants.

Diarrhea

Schnoodle puppies have sensitive digestive systems that can be upset by any disruption in their diet, from eating human food to getting into the garbage. This will result in diarrhea (watery and frequent bowel movements).

Typically, an instance of diarrhea caused by one of these factors will resolve on its own within 24 hours after the offending food has passed out of the animal's system.

During episodes of diarrhea, give your puppy only small amounts of dry food and do not include any treats. It is imperative the puppy has access to fresh, clean water. If the condition has not improved in 24 hours, take the dog to the vet.

Even adult dogs will sometimes have occasional gastrointestinal upsets that manifests as diarrhea. Typically, this is not a serious health concern so long as the episode resolves in a day. Any chronic or prolonged condition, however, is another matter.

For chronic, episodic diarrhea, the cause is typically dietary and often linked to an overabundance of rich, fatty food. Try switching to a food that is lower in fat, with less protein. Smaller portions and more frequent feedings are also indicated.

If you suspect that the cause of the upset is an allergy, consider having your dog tested so you can find the right food. Many small dogs are allergic to chicken and turkey, for instance.

There is always the possibility that the diarrhea is being caused by some pathogen, either a bacteria or a virus. If vomiting and a fever are also present, your pet is likely suffering from an infection and requires veterinary attention.

Finally, your dog may need to be wormed. Both tapeworm and roundworm can cause instances of diarrhea.

Photo Credit: Amie Thorgerson of Simply Schnoodles

Vomiting

Vomiting, like diarrhea, may also be a sign of a change in diet or an indication that the puppy has gotten into something that didn't agree with him. So long as your dog is actually throwing up and getting the substance out of his system, the issue should resolve in about 24 hours.

However, if the dog is attempting to vomit and cannot expel anything, if there's any trace of blood in the material that is expelled, or if your pet cannot even keep water down, call the vet immediately. Dehydration is a dangerous and potentially fatal condition and may require the administration of intravenous fluids.

Always examine the area where your Schnoodle has been and try to identify anything with signs of chewing or any item that is missing and might have been swallowed. This may help both you and the vet to get a handle on the cause of the dog's illness.

Other potential causes of vomiting include the presence of hookworm or roundworm, pancreatitis (inflammation of the pancreas), diabetes, thyroid disease, kidney disease, liver disease or some sort of physical obstruction that has caused a blockage. In this latter instance, surgery may be necessary.

In cases of both diarrhea and/or vomiting, you can add white rice to your Schnoodle's regular food after 48 hours to improve the consistency of the stools and to settle ongoing stomach upset. Generally, you can resume your pet's regular diet after 72 hours.

Allergies

Schnoodles of any age can suffer from allergies. These may be either environmental or caused by substances like cleaning solutions, laundry soap or fabric softeners. Puppies come into contact with this type of chemical most often in their bedding, but they can also rub against things in your home and be exposed to the irritant.

Typical canine responses to allergic reactions include scratching, licking and chewing, but this behavior will differ from a response to fleas. With fleas, the dog will scratch or chew intermittently, but with allergies, they will worry at the spot constantly, often causing patches of hair loss and the eruption of skin rashes.

If possible, identify and remove the irritants causing the problem. Begin by washing your dog's bedding in perfume-free detergent, and do not use dryer sheets. If anything new has come into the house against which the dog might be rubbing, temporarily remove the item. Also, if you have switched to a new brand or flavor of food, go back to what the puppy was eating previously.

In instances where you cannot discover the source of the irritation, it may be necessary to take your Schnoodle in for allergy testing. It is possible your pet will need antihistamines to provide relief and stop the chewing and scratching.

Heartworms

Heartworms are thin, long worms that live in the cardiac muscle and cause bleeding and blocked blood vessels. The presence of these parasites can lead to heart failure and death. Coughing and fainting, as well as an intolerance to exercise, are all symptoms of heartworm. The parasite, *Dirofilaria Immitis,* is transmitted by a mosquito bite. You should discuss heartworm prevention with your vet and, together, decide on the best course of action to keep your pet safe.

Bad Breath and Dental Care

While bad breath or halitosis is not a health problem per se, it can be an indication of dental issues, like an over-accumulation of plaque or periodontal disease like gingivitis. Regular dental exams by the vet and brushing your pet's teeth daily will help to prevent these problems.

Your vet's office should carry "finger brushes," canine-specific toothpaste and dental chews. Using these products does not replace regular dental cleanings, but they are very helpful. Ask your vet to demonstrate the proper way to brush your dog's teeth and start early. Puppies are much more agreeable to the process than older dogs.

Other problems that may lead to bad breath include sinus infections, canine diabetes, tonsillitis, respiratory disease, kidney disease, liver disease, gastrointestinal blockages and even cancer. Always consult with your vet in instances of chronic and unresolved halitosis.

Other Warning Signs

Often, the signs of serious illness are subtle. Again, trust your instincts. You know your Schnoodle. If you think something is wrong, do not hesitate to consult with your vet. Lookout for:

- Excessive and unexplained drooling
- Excessive consumption of water and increased urination
- Changes in appetite leading to weight gain or loss
- Marked change in levels of activity
- Disinterest in favorite activities
- Stiffness and difficulty standing or climbing stairs
- Sleeping more than normal
- Shaking of the head
- Any sores, lumps or growths
- Dry, red or cloudy eyes

Anal Glands

If your Schnoodle has an episode of diarrhea, or if the animal's stools tend to be soft, the sacs on either side of the anus, the anal glands, may become blocked and foul smelling.

Signs that a dog has blocked anal glands typically include scooting or rubbing the bottom on the ground or carpet. If this occurs, the glands will need to be expressed by a veterinarian to prevent an abscess from forming.

Natural Products for Your Schnoodle

In the long run, it's much easier and less costly to practice preventative medicine than to treat illness and disease. Nature provides many beneficial properties from plant extracts.

Aloe Vera

A plant that is used for pain relief and to promote skin recovery from burns, aloe vera is great for relieving irritated skin because it contains anti-inflammatory and anti-bacterial agents that prevent infections.

Chamomile

This is used frequently in aromatherapy and originated from the flowers in chamomile plants. Used as a pain reliever, muscle relaxant, stress reducer and skin healing accelerant, this product proves to be a favorite among holistic groomers and pet parents.

Colloidal Oatmeal

"Colloidal" means that all the oats are finely processed into a powder, thus allowing suspension within the product. The small particles then will coat your Schnoodle's skin and provide an FDA-approved anti-itch and fantastic skin healing formula.

Neem Oil

This extract is derived from seeds and the nuts of the neem tree and destroys pests such as fleas, mites, and ticks.

Jojoba Oil

This unique and natural oil is derived from the Jojoba plant. It tends to moisturize both your Schnoodle's skin and coat, and also provides natural and organic healing properties.

Shea Butter

Shea butter is extracted from the bean or seed of the karate tree, which is native to Africa. Shea butter is a wonderfully gentle and hydrating product that soothes skin irritations and also offers natural protection from the sun's harmful rays. As usual, always contact your veterinarian to discuss herbal remedies before use on your Schnoodle.

Photo Credit: Staley from Melinda Pierce

Chapter 7 - Breeding Your Schnoodle

A responsible Schnoodle breeder will only breed with the most temperamentally sound and healthiest Schnoodles. These traits must come from both parents. Only Schnoodle puppies that are free from any genetic disorders should be used to breed.

Photo Credit: Amy Dillabough of A & R Country Kennel

Responsible breeders will keep records of all the lineage of both parents, such as physical characteristics, colors, sizes and genetic health issues. Good breeders will keep records of pups that have been sold as pets and those that have been sold for show or potential breeding stock.

Schnoodles could be predisposed to certain eye conditions, hip dysplasia and skin disorders.

Schnoodles that are first generation (F1 Schnoodles) have bloodlines that have been outcrossed. They are never inbred, because two distinctly different types of dogs have been used. Thus, there could never be any inbreeding.

With F1 Schnoodles, you won't see the typical problems that purebred Schnoodles face. The first new generations used to breed are the healthiest and hardly have any inherited faults.

Photo Credit: Stuart from Jennifer Sturgeon

Hybrid vigor in the breeding sense means that the gene pool has been renewed. In this case, the problems that would be inherent in the parent breeds would have very little chance of being passed on in the gene pool of the offspring. This is because the genes responsible for certain conditions are not the same in every breed of dog. Thus, the genes don't combine to carry the medical condition in the new litter of Schnoodle puppies.

If the very best Schnoodles are used for breeding, the puppies should be healthy and free of any conditions. What is most important is the quality of care that the mother Schnoodle receives during pregnancy and during lactation.

Good care must be given to both Schnoodle mother and puppies after birth as well to ensure that everyone stays healthy.

Crossing a Poodle With a Miniature Schnauzer

• There are many qualities that can be determined such as color, size and temperament.

• Poodles can be three sizes. If you breed a small Toy Poodle with a very small female Miniature Schnauzer, this would result in miniature, toy-size Schnoodle puppies.

• You could also do this for larger Schnoodle puppies and breed a Miniature Schnauzer male to a female Standard Poodle. The puppies from this litter would most likely be larger puppies.

• In all litters, some puppy sizes will vary due to many Toy and Miniature Poodles having been cross-bred over many years.

• Female Schnoodles come into season every 6 months.

• Females will carry puppies for 57-63 days.

• Female Miniature Schnauzers may carry for as long as 76 days.

• Breeding means dedication, responsibility and effort.

Chapter 8 - Preparing for Older Age

It can be heartbreaking to watch your beloved pet grow older – he may develop health problems like arthritis, and he simply might not be as active as he once was. All you can do is learn how to provide for your Schnoodle's needs as he ages so you can keep him with you for as long as possible.

Photo Credit: Beth and Eric Krueger of California Schnoodles

What to Expect

Aging is a natural part of life for both humans and dogs. Unfortunately, dogs reach the end of their lives sooner than most humans do. Once your Schnoodle reaches the age of 8 years or so, he can be considered a "senior" dog.

At this point, you may need to start feeding him a dog food specially formulated for older dogs, and you may need to take some other precautions as well.

In order to properly care for your Schnoodle as he ages, you might find it helpful to know what to expect:

• Your dog may be less active than he was in his youth – he will likely still enjoy walks, but he may not last as long as he once did and he might take it at a slower pace.

• Your Schnoodle's joints may start to give him trouble – check for signs of swelling and stiffness, and consult your veterinarian with any problems.

• Your dog may sleep more than he once did – this is a natural sign of aging, but it can also be a symptom of a health problem, so consult your vet if your dog's sleeping becomes excessive.

• Your dog may have a greater tendency to gain weight – this is particularly common in smaller breeds like the Schoodle, so you will need to carefully monitor his diet to keep him from becoming obese in his old age.

• Your dog may have trouble walking or jumping.

• Your dog's vision may no longer be as sharp as it once was.

• You may need to trim your Schnoodle's nails more frequently if he doesn't spend as much time outside as he once did when he was younger.

• Your dog may be more sensitive to extreme heat and cold, so make sure he has a comfortable place to lie down both inside and outside.

• Your dog will develop gray hair around the face and muzzle – this may be less noticeable in Schnoodles with a lighter coat.

While many of the signs mentioned above are natural side effects of aging, they can also be symptoms of serious health conditions. If your dog develops any of these problems suddenly, consult your veterinarian immediately.

Caring for an Older Schnoodle

When your Schnoodle gets older, he may require different care than he did when he was younger.

The more you know about what to expect as your Schnoodle ages, the better equipped you will be to provide him with the care he needs to remain healthy and mobile.

Below you will find some tips for caring for your Schnoodle dog as he ages:

• Schedule annual visits with your veterinarian to make sure your Schnoodle is in good condition.

• Consider switching to a dog food that is specially formulated for senior dogs – a food that is too high in calories may cause your dog to gain weight.

• Supplement your dog's diet with DHA and EPA fatty acids to help prevent joint stiffness and arthritis.

• Brush your Schnoodle's teeth regularly to prevent periodontal diseases, which are fairly common in older dogs.

• Continue to exercise your dog on a regular basis – he may not be able to move as quickly, but you still need to keep him active to maintain joint and muscle health.

• Provide your Schnoodle with soft bedding on which to sleep – the hard floor may aggravate his joints and worsen arthritis.

• Use ramps to get your dog into the car and onto the bed, if he is allowed, because he may no longer be able to jump.

• Consider putting down carpet or rugs on hard floors – slippery hardwood or tile flooring can be problematic for arthritic dogs.

Elderly dogs are also likely to exhibit certain changes in behavior, including:

• Confusion or disorientation
• Increased irritability
• Decreased responsiveness to commands
• Increase in vocalization (barking, whining, etc.)
• Heightened reaction to sound
• Increased aggression or protectiveness
• Changes in sleep habits
• Increase in house soiling accidents

As your Schnoodle ages, these tendencies may increase – he may also become more protective of you around strangers.

The most important thing you can do for your senior dog is to schedule regular visits with your veterinarian. You should also, however, keep an eye out for signs of disease as your dog ages.

The following are common signs of disease in elderly dogs:

• Decreased appetite

- Increased thirst and urination
- Difficulty urinating/constipation
- Blood in the urine
- Difficulty breathing/coughing
- Vomiting or diarrhea
- Poor coat condition

If you notice your elderly Schnoodle exhibiting any of these symptoms, you would be wise to seek veterinary care for your dog as soon as possible.

Euthanasia

End of life decisions for our pets are some of the toughest choices any animal lover can make. No one can or should tell you what to do in this regard.

At those times when I have had to make the choice to aid a pet into a peaceful and pain-free transition, I have been extremely fortunate to have the advice and counsel of veterinary professionals who cared about me as well as my animal.

I can't emphasize strongly enough how important it is to have a vet you trust and with whom you can talk. My vet cared for me as much as she cared for my dogs and cats, and knew that I had one criterion in making my health care decisions — is the animal suffering and is there anything you can do to help?

I will confess I have gone to financial extremes in caring for my animals, and I have witnessed others do the same.

For the most part, our pets don't know when they have a fatal illness, nor do they mourn the passing of the years as we humans do. The great gift of their existence is a life lived completely in the present — and completely present. We often suffer far more than they do.

You must make the best decision that you can for your pet, but from my perspective, that last decision, to relieve the suffering of a beloved pet at the end of his life, is a great act of love. I think they know that.

When the time comes, euthanasia, or putting a dog "to sleep," will usually be a two-step process.

First, the veterinarian will inject the dog with a sedative to make them sleepy, calm and comfortable.

Second, the veterinarian will inject a special drug that will peacefully stop their heart.

These drugs work in such a way that the dog will not experience any awareness whatsoever that their life is ending. What they will experience is very similar to falling asleep, or what we humans experience when going under anesthesia during a surgical procedure.

Once the second stage drug has been injected, the entire process takes about 10 to 20 seconds, at which time the veterinarian will then check to make certain that the dog's heart has stopped.

There is no suffering with this process, which is a very gentle and humane way to end a dog's suffering and allow them to peacefully pass on.

We humans are often tempted to delay the inevitable moment of euthanasia, because we love our dogs so much and cannot bear the thought of the intense grief we know will overwhelm us when we must say our final goodbyes to our beloved companion.

Unfortunately, we may regret that we allowed our dog to suffer too long and find ourselves wishing that we humans had the option to peacefully let go when we reach such a stage in our own lives.

Grieving a Lost Pet

Some humans have difficulty fully recognizing the terrible grief involved in losing a beloved canine friend.

There will be many who do not understand the close bond we humans can have with our dogs, which is often unlike any we have with our human counterparts.

Your friends may give you pitying looks and try to cheer you up, but if they have never experienced the loss of such a special connection themselves, they may also secretly think you are making too much fuss over "just a dog."

For some of us humans, the loss of a beloved dog is so painful that we decide never to share our lives with another, because the thought of going through the pain of such a loss is unbearable.

Expect to feel terribly sad, tearful and yes, depressed, because those who are close to their canine companions will feel their loss no less acutely than the loss of a human friend or life partner.

The grieving process can take some time to recover from, and some of us never totally recover.

After the loss of a family dog, first you need to take care of yourself by making certain that you remember to eat regular meals and get enough sleep, even though you will feel an almost eerie sense of loneliness.

Losing a beloved dog is a shock to the system that can also affect your concentration and your ability to find joy or be interested in participating in other activities that are a normal part of your daily life.

Other dogs, cats and pets in the home will also be grieving the loss of a companion and may display this by acting depressed, being off their food or showing little interest in play or games.

Therefore, you need to help guide your other pets through this grieving process by keeping them busy and interested, taking them for extra walks and finding ways to spend more time with them.

Many people do not wait long enough before attempting to replace a lost pet and will immediately go to the local shelter and rescue a deserving dog. While this may help to distract you from your grieving process, this is not really fair to the new fur member of your family.

Bringing a new pet into a home that is depressed and grieving the loss of a long-time canine member may create behavioral problems for the new dog that will be faced with learning all about their new home, while also dealing with the unstable energy of the grieving family.

A better scenario would be to give yourself the time to properly grieve by waiting a minimum of one month to allow yourself and your family to feel happier and more stable before deciding upon sharing your home with another dog.

Bonus Chapter 1 - Interview with Catherine Wilson

I hope you have enjoyed reading this guide on Schnoodle dogs, and we are not quite finished yet. This extra section is an interview that I did with expert Catherine Wilson.

Catherine, can you tell us a little bit about yourself?

I am Cat Wilson. I have been an animal enthusiast for as long as I can remember. My husband lovingly calls me Ellie May Clampett. We have BHG Farms, which we jokingly say is part of Noah's Ark. We are now Oodles of Schnoodles, part of BHG Farms. We are a very small and selective breeder of Schnoodles and only Schnoodles. We are located in Tennessee, just north of Chattanooga in the Sequatchie Valley.

How long have you been involved in breeding Schnoodles and what made you get started?

We started the process of looking at Schnoodles about 5 years ago when there was not too much information on the breed. We actually started breeding as a home school project to show the value of money and how making money includes hard work.

We very quickly realized what a treasure we had with our breeding! So now our "Mission Statement" is to match amazing dogs with amazing families!

Given your experience with the Schnoodle, perhaps you could enlighten our readers with some insights into how the breed began, whether it is becoming more popular or less as time goes on, perhaps your thoughts on how you see the breed progressing?

I have not found information as to when this breed began. People have been crossing breeds for years in order to get the best characteristics of both breeds. In this case, the Giant Schnauzer and the Standard Poodle.

In the short time we have been breeding Giant Schnoodles we have gone from breed obscurity to extreme breed popularity.

When we first started I had to educate everyone who called on the attributes of this designer breed, but now most people who contact us are very educated on the Breed! Now I only see this increasing with time because of the amazing breed characteristics this dog possesses.

What can a new owner expect in terms of differences between this breed and others?

I used to show AKC Akitas but have much knowledge on many breeds. Over our 30 years of marriage we have bred Labs (both black and yellow for hunting), Great Pyrenees for our farm guard dogs, and Rat Terriers (all on a very limited basis).

I have worked with many other breeds in training and such. I also help people out with their breed and training issues now. I say that so you can know when I talk about breed characteristics you will know that I am in the know!

Sometimes when I talk to a prospective puppy buyer and I am sharing with them just how amazing these dogs are, I feel like I sound like a used car dealer. I feel like I sound like I am telling a fairy tale. I mean, can any dog be THAT good?! The answer is yes!! Both the Giant Schnauzer and the Standard Poodle are breeds that are very intelligent and eager to please their master!

Being eager to please is the real positive here. If a breed is smart but does not possess the eager to please part, there will be issues and battles of the will. That can spell trouble for the average home! Because the Schnoodle is eager to please and is a people/family loving dog, you cannot expect to leave him outside in the yard all day by himself and expect a good dog. This breed wants to be with their humans ... to take care of their (their human's) needs! If you are looking for a family dog, one that is with you in your home, that loves to go places and do things with you, then the Schnoodle could be right for you!!

They are very easy to potty train, obedience train, and train to do tricks or tasks around the home or office. Because of their ease in training and wanting to please their people, this breed is fast becoming very sought after for service dogs (we have had several puppies go into service work for their owners). I describe this breed in one word, grounded!

Why would they choose a Schnoodle over say, a more mainstream (AKC) breed?

There are several reasons I would choose a Schnoodle over a mainstream breed. One, I believe by having a cross breed you actually have a stronger genetic constitution (meaning an overall healthier breed). This breed is the perfect combination of personality (ours tend to be talkers – I do believe, they believe they can talk human!). They keep their owners very entertained, and they're calm! The Schnoodle will love to go outside for a run, hike, play ball, or swim! But you are just as likely to see your Schnoodle curled up at your feet, just enjoying being with you!

A main selling point is the "hypo-allergenic" side of this dog. Most people who are allergic to dogs can handle the Schnoodle coat (we have never had an allergy issues with our dogs and we have had them go to homes with extreme allergies!). Even if you don't have allergies, having a dog that does not shed will equate to having a much cleaner home!!

Can you offer advice to people looking to buy a Schnoodle?

Now that this breed is gaining in popularity you will see many more breeders jumping on the Schnoodle bandwagon to make money. Look for a breeder that not only cares deeply about the breed but also cares about you the buyer, because without that combination you will get a breeder that is out of balance!

If you find one that is passionate about the breed but does not care for the prospective buyer, then you won't have a smooth transition from their home to yours. If you find one that seems to really care for you but is dealing in several breeds, then you are probably looking at a puppy mill.

Do your research! It is when people make snap decisions or when they feel pressured that mistakes happen. So go slow. Take your time. Price is not always indicative of a great breeder! For example, we purposely keep our prices down so that real families can afford our very real dogs! Buying the most expensive puppy is not always the best.

Are there things that you see owners doing that frustrate you?

The more you include your new puppy into your day to day life the better dog it will be. Don't lock it away in the yard or kennel and expect the calm, eager to please dog that this breed is known for!

Do you have any advice on bringing home a puppy, training and settling him into your home?

I feel because this is such an intelligent breed that 8 weeks old is way too young for them to go to their forever new homes. This is the legal age in the USA, but just because it is the legal minimum does not mean it is the best (this is especially true for the Giant or large breeds). The short time between 8 weeks and 10-12 weeks will make all the difference in a smooth transition from the breeder's home to your home. During the 2-4 weeks, there are several things that happen: the Mom or Dam of the litter will do much discipline to the puppies, teaching them a pecking order and manners!

Also, during this time their brain does a lot of maturing. By waiting, your baby will be much more ready to sleep on their own (you won't have those horrible sleepless nights due to a puppy crying all night), they will also be much more ready to potty train. Their bladder will be able to hold all night long.

We also make sure that each of our puppies goes home with a blanket and a plush toy that smells like us and their mom and litter mates. This is another great tool for transition.

What would be the positives and negatives of owning a Schnoodle would you say?

The positives very much outweigh the negatives. The only negative that I can see is that they are a dog that needs to be groomed. They have hair rather than fur. So if you don't groom them yourself that will be an extra expense. But it is because of them having hair and not fur which makes them not shed or be an allergen to their owners.

So now that we got that out of the way, here is a list of positives (although certainly not exhaustive). They are smart, funny, active yet calm, clean, hypoallergenic, easy to train the basics and tricks, great companion, not yappy yet a good watch dog, impressive looks, just an all-around great dog!!

Are there particular health issues owners should be aware of?

Because they are a cross bred dog, I believe they have a stronger health outlook. We have not encountered any breed health issues at all.

What feeding routines and types of food/supplements do you recommend?

I highly recommend that pet owners (all pet owners of any animal) not feed GMO. For dogs and cats that means reading the label. Look for corn, soy and wheat (wheat is not GMO but it is a big allergen); if that is in the ingredients, keep looking. There are good brands out there, you just have to dig. They are usually the more expensive ones but truly it is worth it. The GMOs create inflammation in the body and over the course of your dog's life can drastically affect their quality of life and longevity (how long they live).

Are there accessories that you can particularly recommend owners buy?

A kennel for them to sleep in and have a space of their own. Everyone gets stressed and having their own space to go to is a nice way to alleviate stress. We also recommend a string of bells to hang on the door you want to teach him to go out of.

Schnoodles are so smart you can teach them easily to tell you when they want to go outside. A good leash and thin choke collar for walking!

I also highly recommend my puppy buyers all spend some time watching the Dog Whisperer and watching how he does things. His methods are easily duplicable and effective!

Are there any final thoughts that you feel the readers of this book would benefit from?

If you are looking for the BEST breed of dog out there, look no further! The Schnoodle is it!!

Thanks so much Cat for sharing your expertise and just for sharing your unique story with everyone.

Cat Wilson of BHG Farms
http://oodlesofschnoodles.weebly.com/

Bonus Chapter 2 - Interview with Amy Dillabough

Amy thanks for doing this interview, can you tell us who you are and where you are based?

Hi, my name is Amy. I live in the beautiful area of Bancroft, in Ontario, Canada. My home and kennel is set on 26 acres, with lots of trees and yard to run and play in. I have a 9 year son named Cole. He is my helper at times. He is the little man of the house.

I know you have been breeding Schnoodles for some time, can you tell us how long and how did it all start?

When I first started my business Schnoodles were one of the main breeds I did. So I have been breeding Schnoodles for 15 years now and have had great success with this mix.

What types of people are buying Schnoodles and why?

The people who buy my puppies have done a lot of research, want quality and healthy puppies. But more so, they want security in buying from a reputable breeder. One who they have a relationship with for as long as needed.

The Schnoodle is not recognized by the American Kennel Club, is it a question or issue that is raised by many people?

Schnoodles are mixed breeds, so I can understand why they are not an AKC breed. It doesn't matter to my customers that they are not a registered breed. My customers want happy healthy puppies, not show dogs.

What sort of challenges do you face in mating two different breeds?

I have not had any problems mating two different breeds. I am careful who is bred to whom, for size and age and quality of each dog. I allow my dogs to breed naturally – never force a breeding.

What type of health issues can a Schnoodle have and how do you deal with preventing these?

The issues that I have experienced for the 15 years are Liver Shunts, which is something that is not preventable. The other issue I have had is one Schnoodle had an eye problem, I believe it was a detached retina. Again not really something you can prevent. I use only healthy parents to get healthy puppies. Overall they are a really healthy mix.

We know the Schnoodle can vary depending on a number of factors, what type of Schnoodle is most popular?

The most popular Schnoodles for me are the mini schnauzer bred to the toy poodle or mini poodle. These are the two sizes I have and I can't breed enough of them. The demand is really good. I also have a variety of colors, from blonde, red black, black and tan and the typical salt and pepper colors.

Is it possible to describe a fairly typical Schnoodle so people know what to expect?

A typical Schnoodle is super friendly, very smart, easy to train and very loyal to their people. Some are a little bossy so you truly need to be the pack leader with this mix; you need to establish that you are the boss and you are good to go. This mix has to have a leader.

Can you offer advice to people looking to buy a Schnoodle, and how much do they cost?

My advice would be to be sure you have some extra time to spend with your puppy when he comes home. They do need some social time, exercise and leadership throughout the day in order to establish the relationship. You must give this mix lots of free time to run and play and burn down the energy level. I have a schedule of in and out of crate times for the first week or so. I give a great deal of important information to my customers that works 100% for them and the puppy, which makes a huge difference. Cost varies in different breeders. I sell my Schnoodles for $850 plus tax.

As a breed expert, are there any 'essential' tips you would like to share with new owners?

The best tips for this breed is you need to be a leader, you need to be respected as the leader and you will have an all-around great pet forever. So be prepared for your puppy before it comes home, do classes before your puppy arrives if you never had a dog before. It is important to understand how our pet communicates with us. If you understand this then you will do very well with a mix.

I thank you for your opportunity to share with others this great mix of the Schnoodle.

Amy Dillabough of A & R Country Kennel
http://www.arcountrykennel.com

Bonus Chapter 3 - Interview With Mindi Reinbolt

I think to start, would you mind introducing yourselves.

My name is Mindi Reinbolt and my Schnoodle is Bailey. We live in Uniontown, Ohio with my husband Brett and our mini pig Penelopi.

Photo Credit: Bailey from Mindi Reinbolt

Where did you buy Bailey and how much did he cost?

I purchased Bailey from a breeder in Union, Ohio when he was 5 months old for $250 and he is now going to be 4 years old on 12/3/2014.

What made you choose a Schnoodle?

My husband and I had another Schnoodle prior to getting Bailey that we adored. When our other Schnoodle passed away, we were heartbroken and we had another dog (Bich-poo) at the time that was very lonely. So we started looking for another

Schnoodle. They are such good dogs and are very intelligent, affectionate, and so much fun to be around.

What advice would you give to people who are looking to buy a Schnoodle?

Do your homework. Make sure you are getting your Schnoodle from a reputable breeder and always check to see if there is a Schnoodle in need of being rescued. Make sure you have a yard for them to play in and if that is not an option be sure to walk them daily.

Have you had any health issues since you have bought him?

We have not had any health issues with Bailey since we got him.

What is it like being a Schnoodle owner?

It is a joy every day. He is so fun to be around and even if you have the worst day ever coming home to him makes everything better.

Do many people come up to you in the street and ask what type of dog Bailey is?

When we take Bailey out in public or to events he does get a lot of attention. People always ask what type of dog he is and tell us how cute he is. He definitely is a ladies man :)

Does Bailey require a lot of care, e.g. grooming, etc?

Bailey goes to the groomer every 6 weeks to get groomed. This is a must because if you don't get him groomed his hair will get matted and very long. He looks so beautiful when he gets groomed because his beautiful curls are so white and clean.

What about food and diet for Bailey?

Bailey is on the brand Wellness dog food. He gets that plus a dental chew and veggies, cheerios, or other dog treats during the day.

Perhaps you could tell us a little bit about your Facebook page so people can find out more about Bailey?

Bailey can be found on Facebook at Bailey the Schnoodle Doodle. He always has cute and fun pictures posted and talks about his daily adventures.

Do you have any final bits of advice and tips for new owners?

Be prepared to devote a lot of attention and love to your Schnoodle. They crave attention and love and are happiest when they are being played with or having cuddle time. They also LOVE belly rubs. :)

Glossary

Abdomen – The surface area of a dog's body lying between the chest and the hindquarters; also referred to as the belly.

AKC – The American Kennel Club.

Allergy – An abnormally sensitive reaction to substances including pollens, foods or microorganisms.

Anal Glands – Glands located on either side of a dog's anus used to mark territory. May become blocked and require treatment by a veterinarian.

Arm – On a dog, the region between the shoulder and the elbow is referred to as the arm or the upper arm.

Back – That portion of a dog's body that extends from the withers (or shoulder) to the croup (approximately the area where the back flows into the tail).

Bitch – The appropriate term for a female dog.

Blooded – An accepted reference to a pedigreed dog.

Breed – A line or race of dogs selected and cultivated by man from a common gene pool to achieve and maintain a characteristic appearance and function.

Breed Standard – A written "picture" of a perfect specimen of a given breed in terms of appearance, movement and behavior as formulated by a parent organization, for example, the American Kennel Club or in Great Britain, The Kennel Club.

Brows – The contours of the frontal bone that form ridges above a dog's eyes.

Buttocks – The hips or rump of a dog.

Castrate – The process of removing a male dog's testicles.

Chest – That portion of a dog's trunk or body encased by the ribs.

Coat – The hair covering a dog. Most breeds have both an outer coat and an undercoat.

Come into Season – The point at which a female dog becomes fertile for purposes of mating.

Congenital – Any quality, particularly an abnormality, present at birth.

Crate – Any portable container used to house a dog for transport or provided to a dog in the home as a "den."

Crossbred – A dog whose sire and dam are from two different breeds.

Dam – The mother of a dog or litter of puppies.

Dew Claw – The dew claw is an extra claw on the inside of the leg. It is a rudimentary fifth toe.

Dock – To shorten the tail of a dog.

Euthanize – The act of relieving the suffering of a terminally ill animal by inducing a humane death, typically with an overdose of anesthesia.

Free Feeding – The practice of making a constant supply of food available for a dog's consumption.

Groom – To make a dog's coat neat by brushing, combing or trimming.

Harness – A cloth or leather strap shaped to fit the shoulders and chest of a dog with a ring at the top for attaching a lead. An alternative to using a collar.

Haunch Bones – Terminology for the hip bones of a dog.

Haw – The membrane inside the corner of a dog's eye known as the third eyelid.

Head – The cranium and muzzle of a dog.

Hip Dysplasia – A condition in dogs due to a malformation of the hip resulting in painful and limited movement degrees.

Hindquarters – The back portion of a dog's body including the pelvis, thighs, hocks, and paws.

Hock – Bones on the hind leg of a dog that form the joint between the second thigh and the metatarsus. Known as the dog's true heel.

Inbreeding – The mating of two dogs that are closely related (i.e. mother to son).

Interbreeding – The mating of two dogs of different breeds.

Lead – Any strap, cord or chain used to restrain or lead a dog. Typically attached to a collar or harness. Also called a leash.

Glossary

Litter – A group of puppies born at the same time.

Muzzle – That portion of a dog's head lying in front of the eyes and consisting of the nasal bone, nostrils and jaws.

Neuter – To castrate a male dog or spay a female dog; to render the dog sterile, incapable of breeding.

Pedigree – The written record of a dog's genealogy going back at least 3 generations.

Puppy – Any dog of less than 12 months of age.

Purebred – A dog whose dam and sire are of the same breed; both are from unmixed descent.

Separation Anxiety – The anxiety and stress suffered by a dog left alone for any period of time.

Sire – The accepted term for the male parent.

Spay – The surgery to remove a female dog's ovaries to prevent conception.

Stud Dog – A male dog used for breeding purposes.

Whelping – Term for the act of giving birth to puppies.

Withers – The highest point of a dog's shoulders.

Wrinkle – Any folding and loose skin on the forehead and foreface of a dog.

Index

Printed in Great Britain
by Amazon